PYONGYANG
The Hidden History of
the North Korean Capital

PYONGYANG
The Hidden History of the North Korean Capital

Chris Springer

with photos by
Eckart Dege

Entente Bt.
Budapest
2003

Pyongyang: The Hidden History of the North Korean Capital
First edition – 2003

Published by Entente Bt., Budapest, Hungary
Printed at Timp Kft., Budapest, Hungary

ISBN 963 00 8104 0

Distributed by
Saranda Books
11230 Gold Express Dr., Ste. 310
PMB #101-A
Gold River, CA 95670
USA
info@hiddenhistory.info
www.hiddenhistory.info

To order this book, send $29.95 by check or money order to Saranda
Books. (Please add 7.75% sales tax for books shipped to California
addresses.) Add $3 for shipping within the U.S., $8 outside the U.S.

Collecting thorough and accurate information on Pyongyang remains a formidable challenge. Those who can suggest additions
or corrections to this book are encouraged to contact the author,
c/o Saranda Books. Contributions will be duly acknowledged.

Neither the author nor the publishers can take responsibility for any
consequences arising from the use of this book. Travellers to North Korea
should acquaint themselves with conditions there before their trip. Useful
information is provided by the U.S. State Department's "North Korea –
Consular Information Sheet," at http://travel.state.gov/nkorea.html.

Acknowledgements

The author wishes to thank the following individuals:
Eckart Dege, for generously providing most of the photos in this book and for suggesting additions to the manuscript.
Kim Hae Joong, for his research and interpreting assistance in Seoul.
Thanks also to Andrei Lankov, Sarah M. Nelson, Leonid Petrov, and Balázs Szalontai for reading and commenting on the manuscript. Finally, thanks to Kristiina Soone for her encouragement.

About the author

A California native, **Chris Springer** moved to Hungary in 1991 to learn more about the history of the communist bloc. He has traveled extensively throughout Central and Eastern Europe and edited the city guides *Budapest In Your Pocket* and *Tirana In Your Pocket*. He visited Pyongyang in 1995 and 2002.

Note on transliteration

Korean place names in this book are transliterated according to North Korean convention, as best as that convention can be determined.

Contents

Introduction

A recent satellite image of Northeast Asia paints a poignant portrait. Photographed at night, the vibrant cities of China, Japan and South Korea glow like a constellation of stars. Amidst them, barely discernible, lies the landmass of North Korea. Crippled by power shortages, the country is blanketed in darkness.

Our mental picture of North Korea is nearly as opaque as that nighttime image. But here the darkness evinces not an economic failure but a perverse political success. The North Korean state, the Democratic People's Republic of Korea (DPRK), imposes a draconian policy of national isolation. Attempting to leave the country or to contact foreigners without permission can land the offender in a prison camp. And the few foreigners allowed to enter North Korea are shepherded by government minders and kept segregated from the population. As a result, no other country today is as enshrouded in mystery. Fittingly, the North has inherited Korea's old moniker: the "Hermit Kingdom."

One of the few faint glimmers on this benighted landscape is Pyongyang. As the capital, it is one of the few places even marginally accessible to outsiders. Yet even when seen firsthand, Pyongyang defies expectations and resists easy analysis. The first surprise is the grandeur of the cityscape, with its extravagant public buildings and monuments. Despite an economy in cardiac arrest, the infrastructure appears modern and, above all, well-maintained. The same effort has gone into ordering human affairs: indeed, Pyongyang is so obsessively regimented that it feels inorganic. The untidy business of daily life, from picking up groceries to taking out the garbage, is hidden from sight, no mean feat in a city of 2 million. The multi-lane boulevards stand empty – virtually no private cars are allowed – yet smartly attired police direct the trickles of traffic with military precision. Even the children seem bereft of spontaneity: They march to school in uniforms, chanting revolutionary songs in unison.

None of Pyongyang's peculiarities can be examined without reference to the regime that runs it. Rebuilt from scratch after the Korean War, Pyongyang was the blank slate on which the North Korean state etched its self-portrait. The new "hero city" was filled with fetishistic shrines, a paean to state power. The historical nexus between the city and the regime forms the main focus of this book.

That is not to forget another crucial dimension to Pyongyang's story: its inhabitants. Like the rest of North Korea's 24 million citizens, subjects in an audacious social-engineering experiment, their identities have been subsumed under a regime-defined collective. Their personal experiences and perspectives remain out of reach and are thus absent from these pages. But shedding light on their surroundings, and the events that shaped their lives, indirectly illuminates the faces of North Korea's people – the better to recognize and engage with them once the Hermit Kingdom finally opens its doors.

Background

NORTH KOREA
(DEMOCRATIC PEOPLE'S REPUBLIC OF KOREA)

● Prison camp   —— Railroad
▢ Pyongyang   —— Major road
   city limits

SCALE 1:5,500,000

0 km   50   100

CHINA

RUSSIA

Onsong

Hoeryong

Najin

Mt. Paektu

Samjiyon

Chongjin

Pochonbo

Kyongsong

Hyesan

Kanggye

Kimchaek

Iwon

Dongshin   Duksong

Sinuiju

Huichon

Hamhung

Yongchon

Mt. Myohyang

Yongbyon

Pukchang   Yodok

Hungnam

Kaechon

Chongpyong

Taedong

Pyongyang

Wonsan

Nampo

Songrim

Sariwon

Mt. Kumgang

Sinchon

Sea of Japan

Haeju

Ongjin

Kaesong

**SOUTH
KOREA**
(REPUBLIC
OF KOREA)

Panmunjom

38th Parallel

★ **Seoul**

Yalu

Chongchon

Tumen

Imjin

Yesong

CHINA

RUSSIA

● **Beijing**

N. KOREA

● **Pyongyang**

● **Seoul**
S. KOREA

JAPAN

Tokyo ●

History

Pyongyang milestones

108 B.C.E. The Chinese establish the Lelang commandery in northwest Korea, ruled from Pyongyang.

313 C.E. Lelang falls to the Koguryo kingdom; the Chinese withdraw.

427 Pyongyang becomes the permanent capital of Koguryo.

552 Construction begins on the city walls.

614 Sui armies lay siege to the city; Koguryo submits.

661 The Chinese T'ang and the Korean Silla kingdom besiege Pyongyang. Koguryo finally falls in 668.

918 Wang Gon of Koryo designates Pyongyang the "western capital" ("Sogyong"), and rebuilds and revives the city. It becomes Korea's second most important city.

1010 The Kitan kingdom of China attacks; in 1011 the Chinese burn down the city.

1135 Myochong leads a revolt to establish an independent state in Pyongyang but is defeated.

1231 Invading Mongol armies attack from the north but fail to conquer Koryo.

1360 A Chinese tribe called the "Red Head Robbers" invades but is eventually chased out by Koryo forces.

1592 During the Hideyoshi Invasion (known in North Korea as the Imjin Patriotic War), the Japanese enter Pyongyang. They are later driven out by Chinese forces.

1627 Manchu tribes sack Pyongyang, burning it to the ground.

1894 The Japanese drive the Chinese occupiers out of Pyongyang during the Sino-Japanese War. The city is devastated.

1904 The Japanese occupy the city during the Russo-Japanese War.

1945 The Soviets occupy and administer the country from Pyongyang.

1948 Pyongyang is proclaimed the temporary capital of the Democratic People's Republic of Korea (until 1972, Seoul is claimed as the official capital).

1950 U.S. and Republic of Korea (South Korean) forces temporarily drive the North Korean People's Army out of Pyongyang. Later U.S. air attacks destroy the city.

North Korea milestones

1945 The United States and the Soviet Union defeat Japan in World War II. They divide Korea – a colony of Japan – between themselves, with the Soviets occupying Korea north of the 38th parallel.

Under Soviet administration, communism is introduced to North Korea. The Northern branch of the Korean Communist Party is founded.

Waves of refugees leave the country. By 1948 up to 800,000 have fled to South Korea, many under the threat of class or religious persecution.

1946 Major industries, transport, and banks are nationalized.

The Soviets hand over the country's administration to a provisional government headed by Kim Il Sung.

1948 The North Korean state – the Democratic People's Republic of Korea (DPRK) – is founded.

Kim Il Sung becomes premier.

Soviet forces withdraw from North Korea.

1950 The Korean War breaks out.

North Korean forces capture most of South Korea.

United Nations forces, led by the United States, counterattack and occupy most of North Korea.

Chinese forces enter the war on the North Korean side.

1951 The front stabilizes near the 38th parallel.

1952 UN air bombings of North Korea reach their peak.

Soviet soldiers withdrawing

1948

1950

Wartime evacuation of civilians

1953 The Korean War ends in a stalemate; North Korea and the United States sign an armistice.
Korea lies in ruins. In the North, 300,000 soldiers and up to a million civilians are dead; another 3 million have fled to the South.
Reconstruction begins, with Chinese assistance.
The "domestic" faction of Pak Hon Yong is purged from the Party.

1955 The regime proclaims a doctrine of *juche* (national self-reliance) in the first struggle against Soviet and Chinese influence.
Famine hits the country.

1956 Choe Chang Ik and others in the Yenan and Soviet factions challenge Kim Il Sung's leadership.

1958 After a major purge, all factionalist opposition is declared to be eliminated.
Collectivization of arable land is completed.
Nationalization of industry is completed.
Chinese forces withdraw from North Korea.
Chollima – the first major shock-work campaign – begins.

1950

U.S. soldiers fighting in a train yard

1962 The Soviets cut off economic aid as North Korea increasingly sides with China in the Sino-Soviet dispute. The regime restricts political and cultural influence from the Soviet Union and other countries.

1967 The Seven-Year Plan fails due to the loss of foreign aid and to increases in defense expenditures. The plan is extended another three years.

1980 Kim Jong Il is publicly announced as the successor to Kim Il Sung.

1989 North Korea's diplomatic and foreign-trade links weaken as communism begins to collapse throughout the Soviet bloc.

1994 Kim Il Sung dies of a heart attack.

1995 Famine breaks out, hitting hardest in the northern provinces. North Korea appeals for emergency foreign aid. Three years later, the regime reports that 220,000 people have died of starvation. Foreign observers believe the death toll to be far higher – perhaps 1 million or more.

1997 Kim Jong Il becomes general secretary of the Korean Workers' Party.

Pyongyang at liberation

At the end of World War II, Pyongyang emerged from 35 years of Japanese occupation. On paper the city had made great strides. Since 1900 its population had grown tenfold, to 300,000, making it Korea's second largest city after Seoul. New districts had been constructed and major industry established. But the veneer of modernity concealed a bitter reality. Pyongyang's development had mainly served the strategic aims of the Japanese Empire and the creature comforts of Japanese officials.

Though hardly impartial, the Soviet liberators, in their eyewitness accounts, speak convincingly of the burden of Japanese oppression. Colonel B.V. Shchetinin remembered that "Pyongyang in 1945 preserved its colonial past to a remarkable degree." The Soviet commander, Chiastikov, pointedly contrasted the clean and well-built Japanese houses in the city center with the Korean lean-tos and mud huts on the edge of town.

One of the most evocative descriptions comes from Soviet journalist V. Perlin, who visited in 1947. He writes:

The streets of Phyöngyang [i.e. Pyongyang] abound in the most sudden and glaring contrasts. Within a few paces of the smooth central streets, we find labyrinths of narrow, gloomy alleys. In the heart of the city, tiny Korean houses with close-barred doors and windows alternate with smart mansions and business buildings, only recently occupied by Japanese banks, stock companies, and other firms. A glittering motorcar may toot frantically and in vain at a stubborn bullock, yoked to an ancient two-wheeled carriage, blocking traffic at the corner. A slender Catholic cross rises from the spire of a Gothic church in the close vicinity of a Buddhist temple. A lady of fashion, in national attire – a wide velvet skirt that reaches to her heels, a short, bright blouse, and ultra-modern hairdress – walks down the street, exactly one step behind her husband, a stout gentleman in European dress. Custom forbids her to walk at his side. Woman's place is in the rear.

A year and a half ago, every eleventh resident of this Korean town was Japanese. A few tens of thousands of Japanese officials, merchants, manufacturers, and police occupied the best districts and the finest buildings in Phyöngyang. Today there are no Japanese to be seen.

Assault from the air

Pyongyang's location in the Taedong River basin gave the city a huge strategic significance. The Japanese fortified the city heavily as a forward base for their conquest of Manchuria. These military installations encouraged the Soviets to site their headquarters in Pyongyang, which, in turn, helped make it North Korea's *de facto* capital. During the Korean War, this infrastructure would also draw the attention of the Americans, with devastating results.

Initial U.S. bombing raids battered Pyongyang's industrial districts but left much of the city center intact. Visiting in late 1950, Charles Grutzner of the *New York Times* described Pyongyang as "scarred" but not "destroyed."

That would soon change. As the ground war in Korea bogged down, and negotiations began, U.S. air raids increased. Ratcheting up the firepower was intended to undermine North Korean morale and force concessions at the armistice talks.

The raids climaxed in summer 1952. Pyongyang was carpet-bombed, strafed, and napalmed without restraint. On August 29 1,403 sorties were launched – the biggest air strike in the entire war. North Korea announced it lost 6,000 civilians in this raid alone.

Ultimately, even the pretense of choosing only military targets was abandoned. In May 1953, U.S. forces bombed the dams north of the city. They intended the resulting flood not only to cut off military supply lines, but also to ruin rice crops and thereby cause a famine.

But these relentless bombardments failed to damage morale; instead, they needlessly ravaged an already wounded city. By the time the armistice was signed on July 27, 1953, Pyongyang was flattened. Ninety percent of the city's buildings were completely destroyed. And most of the surviving residents had fled, reducing the population from 400,000 to 80,000.

The view from ground zero

The story of life in Pyongyang during the maelstrom of U.S. bombing has yet to find its chronicler. Among the few available sources is the testimony of two Soviet correspondents in *New Times* magazine. Andrei Frolov recalled one raid's aftermath:

Twilight fell on Phyöngyang amid pillars of smoke and clouds of dust raised by the explosions. We went to look at the damage. The city had been deluged with bombs. They had wrecked the unfinished new building of the railway station and razed the whole working-class district around – a giant plough might have passed there. Pieces of wall were piled on each other in grotesque confusion. Many of the streets could no longer be distinguished. Overturned tramcars had been flung a long way from the tracks; tram rails stood up on end and lampposts lay on the ground. Bomb craters gaped in the asphalt; the roadways were littered with pieces of mangled human bodies and scattered household effects.

The regime sent women, children and the elderly out into the countryside for the duration of the bombing. Those who remained in the city, and who were bombed out of their houses, built shacks of bricks and rubble, covered with wooden planks. But such shacks rarely survived the next wave of bombings. Even amid unremitting danger, the locals preserved their wit, as Vasili Kornilov remembered:

The resident of Phyöngyang had to begin life in the devastated city by ascertaining which streets could be used without

1953
Wartime shack

1953

Aftermath

danger of being blown to bits by delayed-action bombs, how to reach the nearest bomb shelter, and the times of the day when the air raids usually occurred...

Explosions can be heard almost incessantly in Phyöngyang even when there are no planes, for the whole city... is strewn with delayed-action bombs. At nearly every street intersection you come across the sign: "Sigetan," which means "bomb with a time mechanism." To mark out the danger spots, sappers surround them with empty petrol drums. As often as not, these drums bear a crude chalk drawing of a bespectacled face and the legend in Korean: "President Truman." When they want to warn fellow-citizens of the presence of a delayed-action bomb, the townsfolk do not say, "Avoid that street, there's a time bomb there!" they say "Don't go that way, Truman's there."

For most Pyongyangites, the only relatively safe hideout was subterranean. Thousands of homes were built underground. Party offices, newspaper offices, post offices, and schools all relocated to tunnels or caves. Locals faced these conditions with astonishing resourcefulness, as Kornilov found:

One evening as we were having supper in a restaurant housed in the cellar of a ruined building, the young Korean manager handed us a slip of paper.

"If this restaurant is destroyed," he said, in a businesslike manner, "you can go to our branch which is already fully equipped. Here is the address."...

Nearly all organizations in Phyöngyang function on this principle. Their addresses often change, but their activities do not cease for a moment.

Reconstruction

Bombs did not stop raining on Pyongyang until the day of the armistice. By then, the city had been practically erased from the map. So complete was the destruction that other communist states actually urged North Korea to rebuild its capital city elsewhere.

But Kim Il Sung insisted on rebuilding Pyongyang. His reconstruction plans had been waiting since 1951. And American bombs had created the *tabula rasa* that allowed Kim to build an entirely new city on the ashes of the old. The ruined churches, "capitalist" buildings, and vestiges of Japanese influence would never rise again. "There were many defects in Pyongyang City," said Kim, "because it was built in an uncultured and lop-sided way at the time of Japanese rule."

The new cityscape was fathered by the Soviets. Korean architects and urban planners trained in the Soviet Union, and

1953

**Reconstruction starts at
Central (now Kim Il Sung) Square**

Soviet urban planners descended on Pyongyang. Their work drew heavily from the blueprints of Stalingrad, Minsk, and other Soviet cities rebuilt after World War II.

The city map was utterly redrawn, with sprawling parks, wide streets, and grandiose buildings. But the most sweeping change was in the city's housing. Kim ordered officials to "pull down the shacks inherited from our ancestors" (i.e., traditional single-family dwellings) and replace them with apartment blocks geared to collective living. Initially, temporary barracks-style housing was built. But in 1956 Kim called for all future residential construction to be permanent. By 1960 all citizens were scheduled to move out of temporary housing and into apartments.

The massive construction effort quickly transformed the city. Pyongyang's entire population was mobilized to clear the rubble and level the ground. Labor brigades of students and soldiers worked around the clock, on construction sites illuminated at night. To one visiting foreigner the city resembled a "forest of cranes." Finally, in the early 1960s, Pyongyang's reconstruction was declared complete. But, as Kim admitted, even then "most of the citizens of the capital were still living in shabby dugouts and old-fashioned one-room houses."

**Konsol
("Construction")
cigarettes**

The Kim dynasty

In communist states, cults of personality are nothing new. But Kim Il Sung took the unprecedented step of turning his ancestors into revolutionary figures, then crowning his own son as his successor. The cult of personality around Kim's family turned into an actual dynasty.

Kim Il Sung – The "Great Leader"

At home he is adulated not only as the nation's savior but as an earthly god. Abroad he is remembered mainly as a ruthless tyrant, responsible for unleashing the slaughter of the Korean War. In almost five decades of rule – longer than any other 20th-century leader – Kim Il Sung ensured he would never be forgotten.

    Kim was born on April 15, 1912, into what official legend portrays as a deeply nationalistic family. In the 1930s Kim led a ragtag band of guerrillas fighting the Japanese near the Chinese-Korean border, before retreating to the Soviet Union. (He later claimed that this inconclusive struggle had liberated Korea.) When the Soviets took over North Korea in 1945,

Kim Il Sung

1951

they chose Kim to lead the ruling Communist Party.

The early years of Kim's rule saw rising tensions between North and South Korea – client states, respectively, of the Soviet Union and the United States. Neither Korean state recognized the other, and both claimed the entire peninsula. Kim decided to reunify Korea by force. With Stalin's reluctant approval, Kim invaded the South, triggering the Korean War. The guns fell silent three years later with millions dead and the country in ruins, but with the borders barely changed. Half a century later, the two Koreas remain locked in mutual hostility. Even the omnipotent Kim could not fulfill his greatest dream: national reunification.

Kim took measures to consolidate his leadership in the war's aftermath. Making constant trips around the country, doling out "on-the-spot guidance" to workers and peasants, Kim projected himself as a man of the people. At the same time, he literally put himself on a pedestal, demanding statues and honorifics like "Great Leader." A cult of personality arose around him.

Kim brutally purged the Party of all rivals, real or imagined. Foreign Minister Pak Hon Yong and his associates were sentenced to death on trumped-up charges. Then, in mid-1956, moderate elements in the Party challenged Kim's leadership. But they failed: those among them who did not flee the country were arrested and never heard from again. Purges and political executions would continue to punctuate Kim's rule.

An ideological dispute placed North Korea's two patrons, China and the Soviet Union, at loggerheads after 1960. To shield his regime from this internecine communist struggle, Kim promoted a doctrine called *juche* – national self-reliance – which secured him political independence.

Juche also mandated economic self-sufficiency. Kim's state achieved rapid industrial growth after reconstruction, thanks to the workforce's superhuman efforts (and, ironically, to Soviet aid). But in the 1970s, North Korea slipped into an economic slump from which it never recovered. Limited foreign trade and the primacy of ideology over technical know-how hampered further development.

Remarkably, economic stagnation did not weaken Kim's rule. Thanks in part to his militant isolationism, the regime endured even after the collapse of communism in the Soviet bloc.

■ THE CULT OF PERSONALITY

The television images from Pyongyang after Kim Il Sung's death astonished the world. With Kim gone, outsiders half-expected North Korea to implode like the communist states of Eastern Europe. Instead, its people were seen weeping inconsolably at the demise of their dictator. Although North Koreans are compelled to worship Kim, they have internalized this reverence to a surprising degree. Outside scholars and defectors confirm that popular devotion to Kim is genuine, as was the outpouring of sorrow at his death.

How could North Koreans come to regard Kim as a god? Kim adeptly cast himself as the embodiment of the independence struggle. Furthermore, Kim exploited Confucian ideas of family loyalty, speaking of Korea as a family and positing himself as its father.

Kim's cult of personality has gone through several different phases. Initially – like Eastern European Party leaders – Kim embodied the national communist movement, but as a mere disciple of Stalin, communism's international leader. Thus Kim's portrait was usually placed under Stalin's. Kim remained symbolically subordinate to Stalin even after Soviet forces withdrew – in fact, even after Stalin died.

**Kim Il Sung
and
Pak Hon Yong**

1951

**1970s Kim Il Sung badge
(twice actual size)**

Khrushchev's 1956 denunciation of Stalin and his cult of personality sent the entire communist bloc reeling. Predictably, Kim resisted the Kremlin's new line, while his rivals used it against him. Yun Kong-hum stood up at a Central Committee plenum to denounce Kim's "dictatorial leadership" and cult of personality. It was the only known public criticism of Kim in North Korean history.

This challenge failed. Kim launched a major purge. To insure absolute loyalty, he also intensified his cult of personality and phased out Stalin's. By 1958 his power was unchallenged.

Kim's personality cult took inspiration from the worship of Mao Zedong in China. In 1967 Kim adopted new honorific titles, such as "fatherly leader." After 1970 every adult in the country was obligated to wear a metal badge bearing his portrait. And foreign-language propaganda promoted Kim's theory of *juche* (national self-reliance) throughout the Third World. The titles, the badges, and the export of the cult were all copied from Beijing.

In 1972 Kim marked his 60th birthday. This milestone – in Korean tradition, the crowning point of one's life – became the pinnacle of Kim's personality cult. An enormous statue of Kim was unveiled in Pyongyang. And Kim, who already headed the Party, government and army, assumed the newly minted position of president.

With an iron grip on the present, Kim had a free hand to rewrite the past. In the late 1960s the regime began hailing Kim's long-dead parents and grandparents as "revolutionary" heroes. This effort to create a sacred First Family would shape North Korea's future as well. Kim named his son Kim Jong Il to succeed him.

Kim Jong Il – The "Dear Leader"

The outside world sat up and took note in 1992 when North Korean state radio carried a sound bite from Kim Jong Il:

"Glory to the heroic People's Army!"

What stunned listeners was not the boilerplate slogan, but the very sound of Kim's voice. This sentence was the first – and to date, the only – publicly broadcast speech Kim has ever made.

Likewise, nothing in Kim Jong Il's political career has impressed outsiders so much as its very existence. Kim defied all predictions by maintaining power after the death of his father, Kim Il Sung, in 1994. Even as a national ruler, the "Dear Leader" remains a recluse and an enigma.

The most basic details of Kim Jong Il's biography are clouded by official legend. Kim was born near Khabarovsk in Siberia. But to burnish his nationalist credentials, the regime claims he was born at a "secret camp" on Korea's sacred Mount Paektu. His birth year (officially 1942) is also disputed.

In his home country, Kim is the stuff of myth – a consummate leader working tirelessly for his people. Like his father, Kim is credited with dispensing brilliant on-the-spot guidance and micro-managing every facet of North Korean life.

Abroad, Kim is known as a cognac-swilling playboy. This image, though lacking in nuance, originates from the rare firsthand account of two South Korean filmmakers (see "North Korean Cinema," page 132). And his hands-on leadership has left fingerprints on some of the regime's deadliest terrorist attacks. These include an 1983 bombing in Burma that killed 17 South Korean officials, and the blowing up of a Korean Air Lines jet in 1987.

Kim launched his political career on his father's coattails – or rather, hidden underneath them. He joined the Politburo in 1974. His portrait cropped up alongside that of his father, and his birthday became a national holiday. Around the same time, the media began heaping praise on a vague entity called the "party center."

Not until 1980 did the truth finally out. The shadowy "party center" was Kim Jong Il. He had also secretly been chosen as heir to his father. Kim Il Sung designated his son as his successor to ensure that his policies would outlive him, as Stalin's did not. The regime later propounded a "theory of revolutionary succession" to justify the establishment of a communist dynasty.

The timidity of the transition suggests that part of the leadership opposed the succession plan. Indeed, despite the rehearsed public praise for him, defectors say Kim Jong Il has never truly won most people's affections the way his father did.

Nevertheless, Kim Il Sung groomed his son carefully, gradually handing over day-to-day control over domestic concerns. In 1991 Kim Jong Il became supreme commander of the People's Army, a key position in this garrison state. When Kim Il Sung died in 1994, his son's curiously roundabout promotion continued. Kim Jong Il was universally acclaimed as the new leader but not actually named Party head until 1997.

Post-1994 propaganda crowned the son with his father's legacy, insisting that "Kim Jong Il is becoming Kim Il Sung." But Kim Jong Il cannot boast his father's achievements or charisma. Kim Jong Il's contribution remained a sort of filial service, echoing the filial loyalty the rest of the country was supposed to show the father-leader. As one North Korea watcher put it, the elder Kim was a leader, while the younger Kim is the son of a leader.

But this is Kim Jong Il's strength as well as his weakness. Kim's father bequeathed to him valuable lessons in wielding power and a nation already conditioned to obey.

Kim Jong Il

친애하는 지도자 김정일 동지
The dear leader Comrade KIM JONG IL

Sites

PYONGYANG OVERVIEW
with districts
(Pyongyang map: p. 94)

HYONGJESAN

Mount Taesong (p. 134) →

TAESONG

MORANBONG

SOSONG

Moran Hill (p. 72)

POTONGGANG

TAEDONGGANG

MANGYONGDAE

Downtown (p. 36)

TONGDAEWON

CENTRAL

PYONGCHON

SONGYO

RANGRANG

RYOKPO

Note

Each site is assigned a number, which is the same in the text and on the maps. Sites do not appear on the maps if their exact location is unknown.

DOWNTOWN PYONGYANG

- ② Site
- ⑥ Vanished site, or status unknown
- ① Site area
- Ⓜ Metro station

SCALE 1:27,400
0 km   0.5

Cholima Statue ⑨

Mansudae Grand Monument ⑦

Korean Revolution Museum ⑧ ⑥

Supreme People's Committee HQ

⑫ Yangchon

⑩ Mansudae Assembly Hall

Potong Gate ⑬   Mansudae Street

People's Palace of Culture ㊷

Pyongyang Students and Children's Palace

Sungnyong and Sungin Temples

⑭ Sungri

Tosongrang ㊶

Russian Embassy ⑰

⑯

Ⓜ

Dept. Store No. 1 ㉘

㉓
㉔ ㉕
㉗
㉖

Ice Rink ㊵

⑬ Mansudae Art Theater

㊿

Korean Central History Museum

Party area ㊱

Nam Hill

Grand People's Study House

⑤

④a

② Kim Il Sung Square ①

Changgwangsan Hotel ㊴

Pyongyang City Prison

㊳

④b

③ Korean Art Gallery

Ragwon Dept. Store ㊲

City People's Committee ⑱

Ministry buildings

Sungri Street

Changgwang Hill   Haebang Hill

Monument to Fallen Soldiers of Army ⑲

㉒

㉑ Rodong Sinmun

Haebangsan Street

Ⓜ Ponghwa

Koryo Hotel ㉝

⑳ Party Founding Museum

Pyongyang Grand Theater ㉙

Ⓜ

㉟ ㉞

⑳ Yonggwang Street

㉚

Taedong River

㉜ Soviet Army statue

㉛ Pyongyang Railway Station

Yokchon Street

Otan-Kangan Street

Potong River

Mansu Hill

Sosong Street

Chollima Street

Changgwang Street
Ryumwanson Street

Otan-Kangan Street

㉓ Ryongwang Pavilion
㉔ Pyongyang Bell
㉕ Taedong Gate
㉖ Korean Folklore Museum
㉗ Workers' Apartment House

Downtown

For centuries, this area has been the core of Pyongyang. "Downtown" in this book is defined as Central District, not including Moran Hill, Rungna Islet and Yanggak Islet, whose sites are covered in later chapters.

Nam Hill

1 • Kim Il Sung Square

North Korea excels at putting on a show – and this is its center stage. On national holidays, this square witnesses awe-inspiring displays of power. Thousands of soldiers goose-step in dress parades, backed by an array of fearsome weaponry. Flamboyant floats tout the regime's successes. Civilians bring up the rear, carrying placards, chanting slogans, and waving to the leader on the tribune.

Through such political theater, the regime creates its own reality. The first parade here was held on the day after the Korean War, when this spot was no more than a clearing in the rubble. Amid utter devastation, the regime celebrated "victory."

Kim Il Sung Square was completed in 1954. Reconstruction plans designated this as the city's main square, surrounded by ring boulevards – echoing Stalin's plans for Moscow. In 1987 the status-conscious North Koreans expanded the square to 75,000 sq. meters, slightly larger than Red Square.

2 • Korean Central History Museum

This museum surveys the history of Korea from prehistoric times until 1919. (More recent times are dealt with in the Korean Revolution Museum.)

On display are paleolithic tools and bronze artifacts from the dawn of Korean history. The museum also presents what it says are the first metal type and the first armored ship in the world. Techniques that influenced Japanese culture are highlighted, pointedly inverting Japan's view that it brought civilization to Korea.

The museum recounts the struggle against feudal rulers and foreign invaders. The nationalist movement turned communist, it is claimed, through the efforts of Kim Il Sung's father, Kim Hyong Jik.

The museum opened in 1945 and was originally located on Moran Hill. During the Korean War much of the collection was secretly buried. Nevertheless, American soldiers unearthed and destroyed some artifacts, then gutted the building.

■ PREHISTORIC PYONGYANG

Displayed in the history museum are fossilized human bones discovered in 1966 in Komunmoru, Sangwon County. These remains are touted as proof that the Korean people originated on Korean territory – indeed, in the Pyongyang area – as early as 1 million years ago. The regime claims that Pyongyang was "one of the world's cradles of culture from the dawn of human history."

These "scientific" findings cloak a political agenda: to deny foreign influence and claim political supremacy over South Korea as the nation's birthplace. In fact, most archaeologists believe the Koreans' ancestors came from Siberia and China.

3 • Korean Art Gallery

Opened in 1954, this gallery traces the development of two millennia of Korean art. That trajectory is curious indeed. It originates with 4th-century tomb frescoes and ancient porcelain. And it culminates in oversized canvases of Kim Il Sung and Kim Jong Il basking in the masses' adoration. (These so-

DPRK Foundation Day parade on Kim Il Sung Square

Ministry building

cialist-realist works trace their inspiration back to Soviet paintings of Stalin.)

4 • Ministry buildings

Built in 1954 by Chinese and North Korean soldiers, the imposing buildings flanking Kim Il Sung Square rank among the first fruits of reconstruction. Official literature once boasted of their "majestic and simple beauty." (Today, overshadowed by grander showcase buildings, they go unmentioned.)

Sources disagree on which ministries are now housed here. The most credible account places the Ministries of Defense and Agriculture on the north side and the Ministry of Foreign Trade on the south side. Mounted on the latter building are portraits of Marx and Lenin – the only such homages remaining in Pyongyang since their doctrines gave way to Kimilsungism.

5 • Grand People's Study House

The regime describes Nam Hill as "the most precious place in central Pyongyang." The mystery, then, is why it was left barren for more than 25 years.

The two churches that once stood here were leveled in the Korean War. In their place, the regime planned to erect a socialist-style government building. It would crown the ensemble of ministries below it, uniting Kim Il Sung Square in form and function.

But the usually resolute regime dithered over the plans for decades. Finally, in 1982, it finished construction on the site. Unveiled was a Korean-style structure, stylistically at odds with the socialist square. And though the building dominates Pyongyang's symbolic locus of power, it is not a government center at all. It is the national library.

Kim christened the library the "Grand People's Study House." (In a rare gesture of modesty, he rebuffed suggestions to name it after him.) Inside the entrance hall, a colossal seated statue portrays Kim as an elder statesman (he was 70 years old when it was unveiled).

The library holds an impressive 30 million volumes. But this vast resource is kept bottled up by the regime. According to North Korea expert Andrei Lankov, all foreign publications, save technical literature, are off-limits to ordinary citizens. Even domestic publications more than 15 years old are restricted, to conceal changes in the Party line.

Official sources say the Grand People's Study House functions as a sort of correspondence university. Most likely, the focus is on Kim Il Sung's works, which all adult citizens must spend hours studying each day.

Grand People's Study House

1959

Supreme People's Committee Headquarters

Mansu Hill

The Mansu Hill area also includes Changdaejae Hill, site of the Students and Children's Palace and Sungnyong and Sungin Temples.

In keeping with its Pyongyang-centric rewriting of history, the regime claims that a demonstration on Changdaejae Hill triggered the nationwide March 1 independence movement of 1919. In fact, the movement began in Pagoda Park in Seoul.

6 • Supreme People's Committee Headquarters

Vanished site.

In the 1940s, even as conquering forces came and went in rapid succession, this building remained the seat of power. First the Japanese used it as the capitol of South Pyongan Province. Then the Soviet 25th Army commandeered it as a headquarters. And here convened the North Korean Supreme People's Committee – the Presidium of the Party.

In 1950 U.S. troops rushed here in pursuit of Kim Il Sung. So did journalist Reginald Thompson. He describes what he found:

We urged our guide to lead us to the nerve centre of communist intrigue and power, the Holy of Holies, the seat of the Dictator. He led us in some awe to an impressive building on

the wooded high ground above the city. This was the Presidium. The whole structure was carefully draped with rope netting and interlaced with foliage, almost invisible from the air. On the first floor quilted double doors led from an antechamber to the impressive inner room of Kim Il Sung. There was the long approach, over an expanse of rich mulberry-colored carpet to the massive, carven, polished desk. One imagined the powerful little ghoul ogling his victims as they made this wretched journey. Plaster casts of Stalin and Kim Il Sung flanked the desk, and someone had thought to decapitate the communist leader and had gone off with his head – for it was not there. Heavy black silk curtains, crimson-lined, hung from the tall windows, and but for the headless cast, all was as it had been left by its occupant. The furnishings of the desk were all in place; the deep upholstered chair but recently vacated.

Kim had indeed fled north. The U.S. Eighth Army installed its headquarters in the building, and GIs took snapshots of each other sitting at Kim's desk.

Though rebuilt after the war, the building has since disappeared.

7 • Mansudae Grand Monument

Mountains of evidence testify to the fervor of the Kim Il Sung personality cult. But it suffices to present Exhibit A. The Mansudae Grand Monument was unveiled in 1972, for Kim's 60th birthday. Standing 20 meters tall, this bronze statue of Kim is one of the largest erected to any leader, anywhere.

Proof of the Great Leader's vanity? Not at all, says the regime: It was not the all-powerful Kim who ordered the statue built, but "the people." Indeed, one legend has it that the statue was to stand twice as tall, but that Kim modestly scaled it down to its current size.

In 1977 the regime covered the statue from head to toe in gold leaf. China's Deng Xiaoping arrived on a state visit the following year and was reportedly so appalled by the extravagance that he balked at giving North Korea more aid. Astonishingly, the regime bowed to this foreign pressure and stripped off the gilding. Even "boundless devotion" to Kim, it seems, has practical limits.

< **Mansudae Grand Monument**

The statue depicts a crusading Kim, slicing the air with an outstretched arm. Some foreign reports claim the statue is gesturing toward South Korea, urging reunification. Not so: the statue faces east. As official literature explains, Kim is "calling vigorously our Party and people to communism," pointing out "the road for the people to follow."

Flanking the statue are two granite flags. They are inscribed: "Long Live General Kim Il Sung!" and "Let's Drive out the U.S. Imperialists and Reunite Our Fatherland!" Huge reliefs of Kim that once appeared on the flags were removed, for reasons unknown, in the early 1980s.

Each flag is surrounded by a socialist-realist sculptural group. One group represents the struggle against the Japanese; the other, the building of socialism. More than 150 sculptors worked on the monument.

Since Kim's death in 1994, millions have been brought here to perform a mass mourning ritual. They lay baskets of flowers at the statue's feet. An announcer, his voice tremulous with grief, intones: "Let us bow in respect to the Great Leader Kim Il Sung." And the mourners bow deeply to the idol before them.

8 • Korean Revolution Museum

Pyongyang's biggest museum covers modern Korean history in a collection spanning more than 90 rooms. The narrative starts with the independence struggle, followed by liberation, the Korean War, and the country's reconstruction. One section examines the "South Korean revolution" (or, more properly, the regime's failed attempts to foment uprisings in the South).

Pride of place, naturally, goes to Kim Il Sung. Dominating many displays are the Great Leader's possessions, including his Korean War jeep. And a diorama depicts Kim's guerrillas fighting the Japanese in the Battle of Pochonbo. The Kim-centric approach spans the generations: a new display room covers Kim Jong Il's first years in power.

The Korean Revolution Museum opened in 1972. Its mosaic of "sacred" Mount Paektu forms the backdrop to the Mansudae Grand Monument.

9 • Chollima Statue

Ancient Korean legend tells of a winged horse called Chollima. It could fly 1000 *ri* (400 kilometers) in a day, too fast for any

< Chollima Statue

rider. This legend was harnessed by the regime and saddled with a political agenda. Seeking to jump-start economic growth, officials pressed workers to toil "at the speed of Chollima."

In tribute to the Chollima movement, this statue was unveiled in 1961. A stirring icon of Korean socialism, its image has been stamped onto everything from banknotes to cigarette packs. The statue captures the horse in flight, carrying two riders. The worker in front is holding up the Party's "Red Letter," calling for work norms to be overfulfilled. The peasant behind him is carrying sheaves of rice.

■ THE CHOLLIMA MOVEMENT

Following the Stalinist model, the regime set out to build a self-sufficient economy dominated by heavy industry. But the Korean War had decimated the country's industrial base and labor force.

The regime's solution was the Chollima movement, launched in 1958. Taking a page from China's "Great Leap Forward," wildly ambitious production targets were set. To meet them, industrial workers were put on double shifts. Likewise, office workers and students were mobilized to "volunteer" their manual labor after their usual working hours.

Chollima produced impressive statistics but questionable results. Reliance on unskilled labor resulted in slipshod work. And the movement, like the legendary horse, raced forth too frenetically for anyone to keep up. Its relentless tempo taxed the workers to their limits. In 1960 the regime had to declare a "buffer year" before the next production plan, to let the labor force recover.

10 • Mansudae Assembly Hall

This gleaming marble edifice houses the national legislature, the Supreme People's Assembly. Built in the 1960s, Mansudae Assembly Hall took its current shape in 1984. Theoretically the assembly is the country's supreme authority. But the 18-meter-tall statue of Kim Il Sung on the podium indicates where power really lies. When Kim addressed the assembly in person, the statue behind him must have made an unforgettable impression.

■ DEMOCRACY, NORTH KOREAN STYLE

Time was when candidates to the Supreme People's Assembly

Mansudae Assembly Hall

were routinely elected with 100 percent support and 100 percent turnout. More recently, turnout has fallen, to 99 percent. It's but one of the vagaries of North Korean democracy.

In these elections all candidates run unopposed; voters cast ballots for or against them. Often, electoral formalities are simply skipped: the 687 representatives routinely overstay their terms for years, without explanation.

If the assembly's elections are a charade, so too are its deliberations. It meets for only a few days a year, to rubber-stamp the decisions of the Party. No proposal brought before it has ever been defeated.

11 • Korean National Association Monument

Exact location unknown.

The regime describes Haktanggol as a secret meeting area for independence activists. In this area, say official scribes, "the Japanese imperialists' watch was not strict." They neglect to explain why: it was located in Yangchon, a settlement of American missionaries (see below).

A stone monument, bearing the relief of a tree, marks the supposed founding of the Korean National Association in Haktanggol. The regime claims that Kim Il Sung's father, Kim Hyong Jik, organized the KNA in 1917 and turned it into the largest underground independence movement. It must have been deep underground indeed, for no foreign scholars can find any evidence that it ever existed.

12 • Yangchon

Vanished site.
Improbable as it may seem today, the heart of Pyongyang was once dominated by a settlement of American missionaries. Rev. Samuel A. Moffett founded Yangchon ("Foreign Village") in 1893. The first Protestant missionary to live in northern Korea, Moffett had chosen forbidding territory. Outsiders were unwelcome, as memories of foreign intrusions were still fresh (see "Monument to the sinking of the *General Sherman*," page 119).

In 1904 Moffett hosted an equally intrepid visitor: Jack London. The author of *Call of the Wild* bedded down in Yangchon while covering the Russo-Japanese War as a newspaper correspondent. To evade Japanese travel restrictions, London had purchased a boat and sailed to Korea himself. Other correspondents, confined to Japan, burned with envy as London filed exclusive reports from Pyongyang, describing the first land skirmish of the war.

Establishing a college, Bible institute and other schools, Moffett and his fellow missionaries gave Christianity firm roots in rocky soil. But by World War II, Japanese pressure to practice Shintoism prompted Yangchon's residents to leave the country. The compound's extensive facilities were later taken over by Soviet commanders.

■ CHRISTIANITY IN PYONGYANG

Western missionaries turned Pyongyang into Korea's most Christianized city, the "Jerusalem of the East," where one-sixth of residents professed the faith. The Gospel made the most headway among independence-minded Koreans. In their reading, it promised salvation not only to their souls, but also to their nation.

Christians paid a high price for resisting the Japanese. But they paid an even higher price after 1945 for opposing the Communist regime. Churches were shut down, church land was nationalized, and clergymen fled south. Today, the regime says, only 10,000 practicing Christians are left in the entire country. Most worship only at home.

Mansudae Art Theater

13 • Mansudae Art Theater

Mansudae Art Theater is best known as a venue for bombastic "revolutionary operas." But its construction was inter-
rupted by a real-life drama. In 1976, during a dispute over a
tree-cutting in the truce village of Panmunjom, North Korean troops hacked two American soldiers to death with an
axe. In the tense aftermath, a civil-defense alert steeled
Pyongyang for U.S. retaliation (which never came). Work on
the theater was briefly halted.

The building adds a splash of color to Mansu Hill. A vast
mural of the revolutionary opera *Sea of Blood* dominates the
facade, and rainbow stripes on the upper floors light up at
night.

Next to nothing is known about how ordinary
Pyongyangites regard their city. But we do know they are
genuinely fond of Mansudae Fountain Park. These fountains
in front of the theater are a popular meetingplace and a favor-
ite backdrop for wedding photos. The main sculptures in the
fountains are performing a dance called *Snow Falls*.

■ REVOLUTIONARY OPERAS

The revolutionary opera marks a radical departure in Korea's
performing arts. Traditional opera recounted old legends and
employed tragic, complex story lines. Revolutionary operas,

Pyongyang Students and Children's Palace

by contrast, feature modern settings, uplifting messages, and simple plots narrated by an offstage chorus. But critics deride them as stilted melodramas.

The regime claims that Kim Il Sung conceived the operas in the 1930s. But it seems unlikely he was actually penning librettos in between gun battles with the Japanese. Truth is, the first revolutionary operas were not staged until 1971 and were most likely inspired by similar productions in China.

The five best-known operas employ themes ubiquitous in North Korean art:

- *Sea of Blood* – A mother and daughter join a guerrilla unit to resist Japanese occupation.
- *The Flower Girl* – A farmer's daughter, falsely accused of theft, leads an uprising against an oppressive landlord.
- *Tell the Story, Forest!* – An anti-Japanese guerrilla fighter assigned to a village must overcome the villagers' distrust.
- *Song of Mount Kumgang* – A family separated during Japanese rule is reunited after the victory of socialism.
- *A True Daughter of the Party* – A Korean War nurse gives her life to honor her commitment to the Party.

14 • Pyongyang Students and Children's Palace

Opened in 1963, this was the first of about 150 after-school centers nationwide. Here young people are trained in music, sports and art. (The most talented child prodigies are used to entertain visiting foreigners.) They are kept busy after school so that parents can stay at work until late in the evening.

Indoctrination is another goal: A shooting gallery here used to employ an American-soldier mannequin for target practice.

The building was a spare-no-expense showcase in its day, even boasting the country's first elevator. Today it is outclassed by the Mangyongdae Students and Children's Palace.

■ COLLECTIVE CHILD-REARING

To counter "reactionary" family influences, totalitarian regimes have sometimes taken steps to separate children from their parents. The Soviets and the Chinese experimented on a small scale with collective child-rearing. But only in North Korea did it become routine. By 1966 the state was raising 60-70 percent of the children, and it sought eventually to raise them all. Kim Il Sung declared:

In bringing up children to be Communists, collective rearing is incomparably better than rearing at home. A home is already an individual unit of society within the framework of private property relations. Therefore, children growing up at home may easily develop traits of liberalism and selfishness.

Children typically spend six days and nights a week at nurseries and kindergartens. These centers, like the Children's Palaces, benefit the state in two ways: Mothers can be sent back to work, and children can be inculcated with the state's values. For instance, all of the country's nurseries and kindergartens have a "room for learning from Marshal Kim Il Sung."

15 • Central Church

Vanished site. Exact location unknown.
In a city that once boasted dozens of churches, the largest and most renowned was Central Church. This Presbyterian house of worship was established in 1901 by Rev. Samuel A. Moffett. Destroyed in the Korean War, it was never rebuilt. It figured prominently in Richard E. Kim's *The Martyred*, a best-selling American novel set in Pyongyang.

16 • Sungnyong Temple and Sungin Temple

Sungnyong Temple (built 1429) and Sungin Temple (built 1325) sit side by side on Changdaejae Hill. Both hosted memorial services for ancient kings. What is striking is how differently the regime treats each temple. Sungnyong is venerated as a temple for worship of Tangun and Tongmyong, two kings the regime holds in high regard. Sungin, on the other hand, has been denounced as an attempt "to implant people's minds with blind and servile submission to the royal authority." This temple honored Kija, whom the regime refuses to recognize (see "Tomb of Kija," page 83). Sungin Temple is that rare site whose significance stands at cross purposes with official dogma.

17 • Russian Embassy

Reflecting Moscow's one-time influence, the Russian Embassy occupies a sprawling compound near the city center. Pyongyang's strictly policed order has shattered here in sporadic incidents, as desperate North Koreans have stormed the compound, trying to defect. (The Russians have handed over all would-be defectors to the authorities.) In 1996 one asylum-seeker shot and killed three guards, then turned the gun on himself.

■ IN MOSCOW'S SHADOW

Long after the withdrawal of the Red Army, Soviet influence in North Korea lingered. "In every house, shop and office hang pictures of Stalin and Lenin," wrote a *Time* magazine correspondent in 1950. "The biggest hotel in Pyongyang is known simply as 'the Russian hotel.' For two full blocks around the

Sungnyong Temple and Sungin Temple

Russian Embassy

Russian embassy in Pyongyang every house is a Russian house."

Culture, too, was affected. In the mid-1950s, Soviet books and films on the market outnumbered those made in Korea. And Soviet news got nearly as much coverage as domestic news.

By 1955 even Kim Il Sung had had enough. Why, he asked, were government offices decorated with Russian steppe landscapes and portraits of Mayakovsky? But not until 1962 was Soviet influence sharply curtailed. As relations with Moscow soured, the regime confiscated Soviet publications, dropped Soviet radio broadcasts and disbanded the Soviet-Korean Friendship Society. Similar restrictions were soon extended to foreign culture in general, isolating the country even from the rest of the communist bloc.

Haebang Hill

After World War II, Sogi ("Auspicious Atmosphere") Hill was renamed Haebang ("Liberation") Hill.

18 • City People's Committee building

Today it is inaccessible and unmentioned. But the City People's Committee building (formerly City Hall) once stood in the spotlight of history. On September 9, 1948, Kim Il Sung stood on the balcony here and proclaimed the Democratic People's Republic of Korea.

Before the Korean War, the square in front of City Hall witnessed numerous Communist rallies. But the world turned upside down when UN forces occupied Pyongyang and held a rally here to welcome Kim's nemesis, South Korean president Syngman Rhee. Fifty thousand packed the square, waving South Korean flags and cheering "*Mansei*!" ("long live!"). Some wept for joy. Their liberation had come, and reunification seemed close at hand. From City Hall's balcony, Rhee assured the crowd: "Now all Korean people can live together in peace and freedom."

But that hope was achingly short-lived. The Communists recaptured the city five weeks later. And Kim Il Sung reclaimed his spot on the balcony to give his troops the command: "March south!"

City Hall was one of only three major buildings in Pyongyang to survive the Korean War. The city's main demonstration venue has since moved to Kim Il Sung Square.

19 • Monument to Fallen Soldiers of the People's Army

Status unknown.

A 6-meter-tall bronze soldier, clutching a machine gun, stood on a pedestal atop Haebang Hill. This statue, erected in 1959, honored Northern soldiers who died in the Korean War. Delegations laid wreaths here in tribute to the fallen warriors.

City People's Committee building

Party Founding Museum

But in the 1990s this site was incorporated into the Party area (see page 66) and closed to the public. One longtime foreign resident believes the monument has since been removed – surprising, if true. Then again, commemorating losses does not come easy to the regime. In the official literature, this somber memorial has been eclipsed by the new, more triumphalist Monument to the Victorious Fatherland Liberation War (see page 99).

20 • Party Founding Museum

It is celebrated as the birthplace of the Party. But perversely, this building – a former colonial headquarters – still bears the haughty stamp of the Japanese Empire. Its pyramid roof was modeled after the Diet building in Tokyo.

The regime claims that here, in October 1945, Kim Il Sung founded the Korean Workers' Party. In truth, he merely opened the Northern bureau of the Korean Communist Party, which had its headquarters in Seoul. The Party's head, Pak Hon Yong, was later purged and executed by Kim.

The building served as the Party Central Committee headquarters. Next door is the house where Kim lived in the heady days between liberation and the Korean War. This modest abode is a far cry from the palatial residence Kim later inhabited (see "Kumsusan Memorial Palace," page 106).

21 • *Rodong Sinmun* building

Rodong Sinmun ("Workers' Daily") is the newspaper of the Korean Workers' Party and the official mouthpiece of the regime. Started in 1946, it claims a circulation of 1.5 million, with most copies distributed for free.

Rodong Sinmun sets the editorial agenda for every other news outlet in the country. Its front page has always been dominated by the activities of Kim Il Sung and/or Kim Jong Il. Inside-page stories typically profile model workers, encourage production, and vilify South Korea.

During the Korean War, journalist Tibor Méray lauded the *Rodong Sinmun* building as the most attractive structure built by the regime. It was destroyed in the war and later rebuilt.

Other sites downtown

22 • Sungri Street

For a century or more, this has been Pyongyang's main street. "Chongno Street" (as it was originally known) was a hodge-podge of Western and Asian architecture that formed the city's commercial center.

North of Taedong Gate, this street traversed the Old City,

Sungri Street

Ryongwang Pavilion

the heart of old Pyongyang. Traditional tile roofs marked the homes of the city's well-to-do. The Old City was inhabited exclusively by Koreans, in contrast to the Japanese-dominated New Town.

To honor the withdrawing Soviet forces, in 1948 this street was renamed "Stalin Street." But what began as a tribute later became a symbol of defiance. When the Soviets denounced Stalinism, the hard-line North Koreans defended it even more fervently. Until the mid-1970s, in fact, the regime pointedly retained its Stalin Street. (The street's current name, "Sungri," means "victory.")

So little of this main street was left after the Korean War that the regime started over from scratch. The street was shifted closer to the Taedong River and made wider and straighter. Tiny Albania, a socialist ally, donated the paving asphalt.

23 • Ryongwang Pavilion

The name "Ryongwang" ("commanding a good view") refers to this pavilion's prime location beside the Taedong River. This L-shaped structure dates back to 1111. In 1592 the Koreans set up their army headquarters here to fight the invading Japanese. The pavilion was rebuilt in 1670. Before World War II it served as the main telegraph office.

Taedong Gate

24 • Pyongyang Bell

This historic bronze bell evokes Pyongyang's vanished past. It hung in Taedong Gate until the 1890s. Each morning and evening the bell tolled to mark the opening and closing of the city gates. It stands 3 meters high and is now displayed in a small pavilion. Eight images of Buddha adorn the bell's surface, along with inscriptions detailing its casting. (The bell cracked during a fire in 1714 and had to be recast.) Perched atop the bell are two dragons, similar to the *pulao* creatures found on Chinese bells.

25 • Taedong Gate

One of the city's most celebrated ancient sites, Taedong Gate is virtually synonymous with old Pyongyang. This "Great East Gate" was the city's largest, standing 19 meters tall. It is topped with roof beams painted red and green. Taedong Gate was built in the mid-6th century and rebuilt in 1635.

26 • Korean Folklore Museum

This museum revisits daily life in pre-1900 Korea. The collection comprises clothing, furniture, and musical instruments. Exhibits on traditional farming stress the communal nature of the work (attempting, perhaps, to give communist collective farms a Korean pedigree). The museum opened in 1956.

27 • Workers' Apartment House

Completed in 1954, this apartment block was one of the first built after the Korean War. "National architecture," it was called, though it is hard to see why. The Moscow-trained architect replicated standard Soviet designs. The building's mixed use – four stories of apartments sitting above stores, a post office and a library – served as a prototype for later housing projects.

The question arises: At a time when barracks housing was the norm, what kind of "workers" were privileged enough to move into this exclusive, centrally located building?

■ APARTMENT LIFE

Apartment dwellers in Pyongyang live as communally as students in a college dorm. Up to 10 families share the same bathroom. Major appliances like televisions and sewing machines are common property. Housekeys remain with the superintendent. Housing is not chosen but assigned, often grouping employees of the same institution. Residents commonly bathe in public baths and have their clothes cleaned in neighborhood laundries.

Apartment life not only binds Pyongyangites together; it also tethers them to the leadership. In 1970 Kim Il Sung ordered that loudspeakers be installed in each household in

1954

Workers' Apartment House

Pyongyang. Though billed as a civil-defense tool, the loud-speakers spout mainly propaganda. Because broadcasts are transmitted by cable, not the airwaves, their content can be concealed from the outside world. Such a device is not unique to North Korea. Apartments in the Soviet Union were fitted with a wire-broadcast loudspeaker called a *radio-tochka*.

28 • Department Store No. 1

The Hwasin department store chain has long been a fixture in Seoul's retail sector. Before 1945 Hwasin also had a store in Pyongyang. Even at a mere two stories tall, it was the city's biggest building. It survived the Korean War – one of only three major buildings to do so. But in 1982 it was torn down to make way for the current store.

Department Store No. 1 sells clothing, appliances, furniture, and toys. (One surprise is the department full of dead animals stuffed and mounted as kitsch decoration.) Consumer culture may seem stunted here – no advertising, ossified displays – but this is as good as it gets. "A show-window of our light industry" is what the regime calls this store, and for most North Koreans the window is closed. To shop in stores like this, locals need hard-to-get authorization cards. Food and clothing are typically distributed at workplaces and schools; until 2002 even these basic goods were strictly rationed.

Department Store No. 1

Pyongyang Grand Theater

29 • Pyongyang Grand Theater

The 1960 unveiling of the Grand Theater signaled a new approach to Pyongyang architecture. Until then most of the city had been designed with Soviet help, and looked it. But Kim Il Sung decreed an end to the slavish imitation of the Soviets. Designers were encouraged to add a bit of national flavor to a bland socialist cityscape.

They topped the theater with a gracefully curved hip-saddled roof, evoking an ancient palace. This element has since cropped up on other showcase buildings. But such roofs are merely references to a national architecture that the regime has all but abolished.

Theaters in Pyongyang operate without a schedule or box office. Instead, performances are held on special occasions, and tickets are distributed in collectives.

30 • Yonggwang Street

Taking over the area around today's Yonggwang Street, Japanese colonial officials established their own neighborhood, called New Town. In sharp contrast with the locals' thatched-roof huts, the Japanese erected modern, two- and three-story apartment houses, in styles reminiscent of home.

The Japanese accounted for up to 20 percent of Pyongyang's population. In their exclusive neighborhoods, they enjoyed a comfort and luxury unimaginable for most locals. "When Koreans appeared in these streets," recalls Kim Il Sung in his memoirs, "the Japanese policemen or merchants scowled at them." The good life on Yonggwang Street ended when Soviet troops arrived, evicted the Japanese and snatched up the best houses for themselves.

Yonggwang was originally known as "Station-Front" Street (it runs east from the railway station). In 1954 it was rebuilt by soldiers and, in their honor, was named "Inmingun" (People's Army) Street. Later it was renamed "Podunamu" (Willow), then "Yonggwang" (Glory). It's not clear why a regime so army-centered would revoke a tribute to its men in uniform.

31 • Pyongyang Railway Station

This station was built to cement Japan's rule over Korea. The railway line was laid for military purposes during the Russo-Japanese War. The station was planted on undeveloped land with the aim of building a new Japanese district beside it (see "Yonggwang Street," above).

The Japanese-built transport network relied heavily on the railways. Thus, with the outbreak of the Korean War, this station became a prime target. American bombing raids reduced it to burned-out train cars and rubble. The station was reconstructed in 1958 with Chinese and Soviet materials.

Yonggwang Street

Pyongyang Railway Station

North Korea has only two international train routes: to Beijing via Sinuiju, and to Moscow via Tumangang. Before 1945, a mere six-hour train trip was all that separated Pyongyang and Seoul. But the division of Korea has made that journey unthinkable. (The two Koreas agreed in 2000 to re-establish railway links for freight, but only the South has laid any track.) Even within North Korea, travel is highly restricted. Citizens may not leave their home city without a permit from their work unit, which must be presented when entering or leaving the railway station.

32 • Soviet Army statue

Vanished site.

After the Korean War, the regime shied from expressions of fealty to the Soviet Union. One curious exception was this statue of a Red Army soldier clutching a tommy gun. It was erected in 1957, on the 40th anniversary of the Russian Revolution.

It may be pure coincidence, but this statue was placed near the very spot where a Soviet soldier saved Kim Il Sung's life. On March 1, 1946, during a political rally, a would-be assassin lobbed a grenade at Kim. A Red Army officer intercepted the grenade, suffering severe wounds. Not until 1984 did the regime acknowledge the incident.

33 • Koryo Hotel

This deluxe hotel offers visitors a dose of Western-standard comfort. Only Yanggakdo Hotel can boast comparable luxury.

The sleek twin towers of the Koryo stand 45 stories high. The southern tower is topped with a revolving restaurant.

In 1985, shortly after it opened, the Koryo hosted a historic reunion. A handful of South Koreans were allowed a brief visit with Northern relatives they had not seen since the Korean War. (The South Koreans were not allowed to visit their families' homes.) These were the lucky few. An estimated 10 million Koreans, North and South, have family on the other side yet cannot contact them, even by mail or phone.

34 • Ryunhwanson Street

Vanished site.

Official propaganda blasts this street's construction as a "criminal" sabotage. How could a street be a crime against the state?

The story begins with the 1955 unveiling of what was originally called "Potongmun Street." Kim Il Sung's scribes link the street to his political rivals, the Soviet-oriented "factionalists."

Kim found fault with the street's three-story brick apartment houses. He condemned them as "not agreeable to the sentiments and customs of the Korean people," particularly because of the heating (the buildings probably lacked *ondol*, traditional heated floors). Even after this problem was fixed, Kim ordered that the buildings be torn down as soon as the economic situation allowed.

However, as time passed, everyone forgot about Kim's order – everyone except for his dutiful son. Kim Jong Il "wanted to obliterate even the last vestige of the factionalists' harm to construction and turn the street into an ideal one which would please the great leader." And so in 1979 the subversive street was demolished.

So goes the official explanation. In fact, the apartment houses were designed not by factionalists but by Hungarian architects. Did Kim's opponents really play a role, or were they simply scapegoated? And what accounts for the bitterness of the condemnation leveled at these buildings?

■ CLASHES IN CONSTRUCTION

The rebuilding of war-torn Pyongyang in the 1950s was dubbed a "construction battle." But the real battle was waged within the leadership. Kim Il Sung fought factional leaders for control of the Party, and construction was but one front in the conflict.

Kim accused senior construction officials of "flunkeyism and dogmatism" – in other words, imitation of Soviet practices. Features like wooden floors and high ceilings were attacked as "foreign" abominations "inconvenient for our people."

In truth, Kim favored many Soviet building techniques. His nationalist posturing obscured the real issue: how much material and effort to invest. Decrying "ostentation and wastage" in residential construction, Kim insisted on quantity over quality.

To this end, in 1957 Kim introduced prefabricated housing. Ready-made wall panels could be assembled even by unskilled "volunteers." In 1958 the regime boasted of building 20,000 flats in Pyongyang with only enough material for 7,000. But this was no loaves-and-fishes trick: the flats were merely built smaller. Moreover, their walls were so flimsy, and their assembly so slipshod, that foreign diplomats wondered aloud how long the buildings would last.

Some officials voiced the same concerns. But they were treated as saboteurs. "A comrade has just said that conservatives

Koryo Hotel

firmly stand in our way," Kim told a Party conference. "I suggest that we dump them into garbage bins."

35 • Changgwang Street

After rubbing Ryunhwanson Street off the map, Kim Jong Il built Changgwang Street in its place. The first segment, north of Haebang Hill, was completed in 1980. Here Kim introduced his "new way of city planning": buildings are slender, with varying heights, and placed far apart, to create a sense of spaciousness. Boasting up to 30 stories, these high-rise towers stand taller than all previous housing projects. And the apartments are a roomy 150 sq. meters each.

The regime lavished resources here for a reason: The area houses high Party officials. One of the residents is said to be none other than Kim Jong Il (see "Party area," below).

The second segment of Changgwang Street, south of Haebang Hill, was finished in 1985. Exclusive restaurants occupy the ground floors of the high-rises.

36 • Party area

The area west of Nam Hill appears conspicuously blank on official maps. A firsthand look reveals little more: the main approach on Changgwang Street is barricaded, and armed guards turn away uninvited visitors. This is the Party area, one of the most restricted enclaves of a forbidden city.

The few available photos of the area show mostly low-lying buildings concealed by trees. Here stands the headquarters of the Korean Workers' Party. Here too is "Office Building No. 15," Kim Jong Il's headquarters. The high-rises along Changgwang Street house senior officials in the Party, government and army.

The Party area evinces one of Pyongyang's most curious paradoxes. Though the state's tendrils poke into every facet of life, the centers of state power are deliberately hidden. (The same is true in Beijing, where the Party rules from inside a walled complex at Zhongnanhai.) Surely security considerations alone do not warrant concealing the Party headquarters and other key government buildings.

37 • Ragwon Department Store

Ragwon ("Paradise") Department Store caters to the privileged: Koreans from Japan, foreigners, and the officials who

Changgwang Street

live in the nearby Party area. On offer is a wide selection of hard-to-find food items, clothing and electronics. This store is the largest that accepts only convertible won (available in exchange for hard currency). It is a North Korean-Japanese joint venture.

38 • Pyongyang City Prison

Vanished site.

Successive regimes used the city prison to neutralize their opponents. Those who resisted the Japanese were locked up here, then released en masse just after liberation. The Communist regime renamed the prison the "Pyongyang Enlightenment House." But their idea of enlightenment was decidedly brutal. In 1950, U.S. troops discovered the bodies of political prisoners here. In Donald Knox's oral history *The Korean War*, Corporal Mario Sorrentino recalls how it happened:

We drove to the city prison. A long stone building, it looked like exactly what it was. Inside, the cells were small and empty.... Someone ran in and yelled that a well full of bodies had been found. We dashed outside. At the end of one cellblock there was a circular cement well. It was not deep – well, I don't know, it might have been. It was filled with the bodies of civilians.

Ice Rink

The regime, in turn, accuses U.S. forces of killing 2,000 prisoners here. This claim cannot be verified. But we do know of other instances in which South Korean forces killed prisoners while U.S. Army officers looked the other way.

39 • Changgwangsan Hotel

Finding a semblance of nightlife in Pyongyang is not easy. The best-known exception is Changgwangsan Hotel. Tucked away atop one of its 18-story twin towers is North Korea's first disco. Officially open to foreigners only, it's frequented by the students, diplomats and aid workers of the tiny expat community. (A chronic shortage of female guests dampens the excitement.) Another expat oasis is the hotel's cafe and ice cream shop, a joint venture of Koreans from Japan. The hotel opened in 1975.

40 • Ice Rink

Fancifully cone-shaped, this showcase sports facility is intended to resemble a skater's winter hat. Built in 1982, it was the first indoor skating rink in the country.

41 • Tosongrang

Vanished site.
Rundown straw-thatched dwellings once lined the banks of

the Potong River, where they were frequently swept away by floods. These shacks were built in slum quarters known as "Tosongrang" (meaning "Earthen Bank Corridor"). The regime presents them as emblems of the grinding poverty endured before communism.

Tosongrang slums were located under Palgol Bridge and in Sosong-ri. After the Korean War, Sosong-ri's residents were relocated, and the area was turned into Potonggang Pleasure Park, near today's Chollima Street.

■ WORKING-CLASS PYONGYANG

The regime proudly proclaims today's Pyongyang to be free of slums. Outside experts agree that there are no slums per se. But in this capital of a "workers' state," the working-class areas are nevertheless hidden away in the back streets. Such areas can be found, for instance, in Pyongchon District and in East Pyongyang. Some consist of rows of barracks-style housing built shortly after the Korean War.

42 • People's Palace of Culture

The hip-saddle roofs here, an example of the regime's Korean-style architecture, were modeled after the wings of wild ducks. This cultural center, opened in 1974, hosts concerts, exhibitions, feature films, and music lessons. Recently, an education center detailing U.S. "crimes" opened here.

People's Palace of Culture

43 • Potong Gate

Built in 997, the venerable Potong Gate is a key landmark of old Pyongyang. As the west gate of the city walls, it provided access to the Imperial Highway, stretching from Seoul to Beijing. The gate still occupies a strategic position at the mouth of Chollima Street. But this vine-covered relic confronts the encroachments of the modern age. It has been shunted onto a traffic roundabout and sits in the shadow of high-rise concrete blocks.

During the historic March 1 independence movement of 1919, protesters demonstrated at Potong Gate. Kim Il Sung claimed that he participated as a young boy and saw Japanese police kill demonstrators here.

Potong Gate

MORAN HILL

- **44** Site
- **47** Vanished site
- **55** Site area
- **Ⓜ** Metro station

SCALE 1:16,400

0 km — 0.5

Friendship Tower **67**

68 TV tower

Chongryu Cliffs **55**

Ryonghwa Temple **65**

Yongmyong Temple **66**

Kaeson Revolutionary Site **62**

Choesung Pavilion **60**

Arch of Triumph Square **64**

Chongryu Bridge

63 Arch of Triumph

Kim Il Sung Stadium **61**

Hyonmu Gate **59**

Kaeson Ⓜ

Kaeson Street

Tomb of Kija **58**

Ulmil Pavilion **53**

Pubyok Pavilion **57**

56

Hungbu Guest House

Rungna Islet

Chongum Gate **52**

Seven-Storied Pagoda **50**

Chongryu Pavilion **51**

Taedong River

Moranbong Underground Theater **46**

45

Liberation Tower **48**

Chilsong Gate **44**

47

Moranbong Theater

Shinto shrine

Rungna Bridge

49 Kisaeng Village

Tongil Ⓜ

Moran Hill

Rising majestically above the Taedong River, Moran Hill has long been Pyongyang's most scenic recreation spot – a favored destination for a stroll, a picnic, or a game of Korean chess. The park is crowded on Sundays, which is most people's only day off. The woods provide more than just a lush backdrop: In times of need, locals supplement their meager diets here by collecting edible plants.

Traces of old Pyongyang come alive amid Moran Hill's historic gates and pavilions. These relics were ravaged by battles in 1593 (during the Japanese Hideyoshi Invasion) and again in 1894 (in the Sino-Japanese War). Further destruction ensued in the Korean War. But after the war, while other parts of the city were deliberately paved over, these sites were painstakingly restored.

Like Rorschach tests, descriptions of Moran Hill's pavilions reveal much about the sources themselves. South Koreans wax lyrical about their vistas and nostalgically recall the royal banquets and "moon-viewing parties" held there. North Koreans dress the pavilions in olive-drab, stressing their use as military strongpoints during foreign invasions.

Ulmil Peak, Moran Hill

44 • Chilsong Gate

The name "Chilsong" ("Seven Stars") refers to the Big Dipper, a constellation once revered by the Korean military. The name was seen as auspicious: Chilsong Gate provided access from the north, the direction from which invaders were most likely to come.

Built in 922, the gate has witnessed some of Moran Hill's bloodiest battles. In 1593 Chinese forces penetrated the city walls here to besiege the Japanese occupiers. The roles were reversed three centuries later, in the Sino-Japanese War. Japanese troops here mowed down the fleeing Chinese. The Chinese commander, General Tso, fell among his men.

■ THE BATTLE OF PYONGYANG, 1894

During the Sino-Japanese War, Korea once again became a battleground for its two powerful neighbors. Pyongyang was occupied by the Chinese and then surrounded by three Japanese brigades.

On the morning of September 15, 1894, the Japanese launched a surprise attack on the Chinese garrison. Overwhelmed, the defenders fled down Moran Hill – directly into a hail of Japanese fire. That night, the remaining Chinese left via the Imperial Highway, the only open road out of the city, only to meet the same deadly fate.

Chilsong Gate

Moranbong Theater

Reeling from their defeat, the Chinese withdrew from Korea without further engagement. The battle had equally decisive consequences for Pyongyang. Four-fifths of the city's houses were destroyed. And the population of 88,000 dropped to a mere 15,000 as locals fled the fighting or died from epidemics.

45 • Moranbong Theater

One of North Korea's first showcase buildings, Moranbong Theater was unveiled in 1946. Its neo-classical facade captures the pomp of Soviet architecture. Kim Il Sung might well have been thinking of these colonnades when he complained: "Some of our public buildings look like garages, and quite a few of them just have huge porticoes and are entirely lacking in utility."

Much of the high drama on this stage has been acted out by politicians. In 1948 the theater hosted the North-South Joint Conference (see page 118) and the opening session of the Supreme People's Assembly.

Korean War bombing raids reduced the building to rubble. "All that is left of Moranbong Theater is two walls facing each other," wrote journalist Tibor Méray. "One can walk through the theater as if it were an open space." Reconstructed in 1954, it is now the main venue for orchestral concerts.

46 • Moranbong Underground Theater

With Moranbong Theater ravaged by American air raids, this theater was built in 1951 to take its place. Lying 250 meters beneath Moran Hill, it was used as a bombproof conference hall and government shelter.

Supervising the theater's construction was former army corps commander Mu Chong. Scapegoated for leading the wartime retreat from Pyongyang, Mu was demoted to this assignment.

Traumatized by the war, the regime went on to build numerous underground shelters. Indeed, the city's entire reconstruction was informed by a lingering bunker mentality. "I say to my comrades that they should not think they can keep our nice theaters and things as they are now," Kim Il Sung told journalist Wilfred Burchett in 1967. "It is possible that all this will be destroyed if war breaks out."

47 • Shinto shrine

Vanished site.

Before Kim Il Sung worship, there was Shinto worship. Shinto, Japan's national religion, was imposed on Korea during colonial rule. Shinto shrines were erected in places where natural beauty was seen as divine. Japanese worshippers would walk through a *torii* (ceremonial gateway) and stand before a tile-roofed shrine. There they would bow and pray to their emperor. After 1937 this ritual was forced on Koreans as well. But for them it was a humiliation, a mark of foreign domination. Some Christians refused to participate on religious grounds and were arrested. After Korea's liberation, the Pyongyang shrine was burned to the ground.

48 • Liberation Tower

Standing 30 meters tall, this slender, star-topped obelisk honors the Soviets who defeated the Japanese occupiers. The tower was erected in 1946, one year after liberation. During the Korean War, it was surrounded by the barrels of anti-aircraft guns, poised to shoot down American planes.

In addition to thanking the Red Army, one of the bronze plaques used to praise Generalissimo Stalin. But the Stalin tribute was removed as politically incorrect when Khrushchev was invited to North Korea in 1959. For months the entire

< Liberation Tower

city was spruced up in anticipation of the Soviet leader's visit; the regime was outraged when he abruptly declined the invitation.

The tower's Russian and Korean inscriptions still hail the Soviet liberation and Soviet-Korean friendship. But time has tarnished these lofty words. Relations soured in the 1960s and never fully recovered. In 1985, during a rapprochement, the regime rebuilt and enlarged this monument. But the gesture rang hollow: The regime had already erased the Soviet liberators from its history books. Kim Il Sung is credited with singlehandedly defeating the Japanese.

■ THE SOVIET OCCUPATION

The Soviet Union occupied northern Korea almost as an afterthought, during mop-up operations against the crumbling Japanese Empire in the last week of World War II. Assaults on Korean ports began on August 10. Most of the fighting was confined to the sea or the air; the only major land battle was at Chongjin. Ignoring their government's capitulation, die-

Relaxing on Moran Hill

1957

Chongum Gate

hard Japanese soldiers fought on until August 20. The campaign for Manchuria and Korea claimed 1500 Soviet lives.

The Soviets came as liberators but quickly became predators. Undisciplined troops looted stores, robbed wristwatches, and even committed gang rapes. On occasion, Koreans fought back with their fists, but the Soviets' overwhelming firepower discouraged armed resistance. In November 1945 an anti-Communist protest in Sinuiju turned bloody when Red Army soldiers fired on the demonstrators.

The very size of the Soviet deployment – some 40,000 troops – made them an intimidating presence, as U.S. official Edwin Pauley noted during a 1946 visit. "While walking up and down the streets of Pyongyang," Pauley jotted in his diary, "I noticed that the most habitable houses seem to be occupied by Soviet officers and their wives." Ironically, Pauley remarked, the Soviets had seized North Korea with lend-lease trucks and guns – American equipment.

49 • Kisaeng Village

Vanished site.
Kyongsang Valley has never lived down its decadent past. Here stood the Kisaeng Village, scorned by today's regime as an "ugly" "amusement center for bureaucrats and other ruling circles." At the taverns here, submissive *kisaeng* (Korean geishas) poured hard drink for big spenders. The lithe young women entertained with song and dance – and sometimes more. *Kisaeng* often served as courtesans.

Visiting the Kisaeng Village, Kim Il Sung was outraged by its hedonism. He had this type of fun outlawed in 1946. Though

Ulmil Pavilion

Kim couched his edict in the rhetoric of women's liberation, he faced spirited protests from the *kisaeng* themselves.

In the same valley-of-ill-repute, Moranbong Youth Park opened in 1959. The park, according to a defector, once held social dances for couples. *This* type of fun was outlawed in 1965, when all but "revolutionary" group dancing was banned.

50 • Seven-Storied Stone Pagoda of Hongbok Temple

A classic feature of the Korean landscape is the pagoda, a tower that stands near Buddhist temples and contains holy relics. This 11th-century pagoda is a significant vestige of the late Koryo Kingdom. The hexagonal tower stands more than 5 meters high, and reliefs of Buddha decorate its granite face. The pagoda was brought to Moran Hill in 1933. Before that, it stood beside the now-vanished Hongbok Temple, in what is now Pyongchon-dong, Pyongchon District.

51 • Chongryu Pavilion

Chongryu Pavilion was originally the upper story of Chonghae Gate, the now-disappeared "Gate of the Calm Sea." The pavilion was moved and rebuilt in 1716.

52 • Chongum Gate

Although it has never been as celebrated as the others, Chongum is one of only five surviving city gates. It was built in the mid-6th century and rebuilt in 1714. Chongum Gate served as the gateway to the Taedong River ferry below the Chongryu Cliffs.

53 • Ulmil Pavilion

Perched on Ulmil Hill, this fabled pavilion offers a sweeping view of the city. The pavilion served as a military command post during the Koguryo Dynasty; later, during the Hideyoshi Invasion, it became a Japanese strongpoint. It was rebuilt in 1714.

54 • Yongwang Pavilion

Exact location unknown.

This pavilion witnessed historic events during Japan's 1592 invasion. Legend has it that, in an act of resistance, a *kisaeng* (Korean geisha) named Kye Wol Hyang grabbed a Japanese general here and leapt into the Taedong River below, killing them both. During the Chinese siege of the city, it was from here that the Japanese army command led a retreat.

Yongwang Pavilion

55 • Chongryu Cliffs

These 2-kilometer-long cliffs form the eastern face of Moran Hill. The name "Chongryu" ("Blue Stream") refers to the nearby Taedong River. Kumnung Tunnel runs through these cliffs.

Before 1910, high officials customarily had their names carved into the cliffs. The practice came under fire years later for the way it "squandered money." The critic of self-aggrandizement? Kim Il Sung.

56 • Hungbu Guest House

This villa enjoys a picturesque location overlooking the Taedong River. The two-story house is topped with a traditional roof of green tiles.

Foreign delegations overnighting here have included some of Kim Il Sung's best-known guests – fellow strongmen Fidel Castro and Muammar Qaddafi. One of Hungbu's recurring visitors was Romanian president Nicolae Ceausescu.

■ THE ROMANIAN CONNECTION

Nicolae Ceausescu's 1971 trip to China and North Korea had fateful consequences for how he ruled Romania. He was deeply impressed with the transformation that Pyongyang had undergone since his last visit seven years earlier. Greeted by mass rallies and guided around grand monuments, Ceausescu came away convinced he had seen the future of socialism. Returning home, he followed in Mao and Kim Il Sung's footsteps. He launched a "mini-cultural revolution" to root out Western influence, and he intensified his personality cult.

Ceausescu would visit North Korea three more times. Pyongyang's bombastic buildings and oversized boulevards, say some observers, inspired Ceausescu's own notorious urban-renewal project. An entire residential district of Bucharest was bulldozed to make way for a gigantic (and, many say, hideous) administrative center. Pyongyang's influence is difficult to pinpoint, but there *is* an intriguing similarity between Bucharest's House of the People and Kumsusan Memorial Palace (see page 106).

57 • Pubyok Pavilion

Pubyok Pavilion originally formed part of Yongmyong Temple. In times of war, the pavilion was used as a command post.

This ancient structure, which dates back to 393, was burned down by the Japanese invaders and rebuilt in 1614. Destroyed again in the Korean War, it was rebuilt in 1957.

58 • Tomb of Kija

Vanished site.
This site was once so revered that those passing by on horseback were obliged to dismount. Here stood a tomb and, nearby, a temple dedicated to Kija. According to tradition, Kija founded a kingdom in Korea around 1000 B.C.E. But scholars now believe his tomb actually dates from the 12th century.

The very existence of Kija remains open to question. Nevertheless, Koreans long cherished his legend. Not so the regime. Because Kija came from China, he represents a foreign influence that official histories reject out of hand. The regime alleges Kija was invented by the Japanese. The authorities opened his tomb, declared it to be empty and destroyed it.

59 • Hyonmu Gate

In the 1894 Battle of Pyongyang, Japanese forces scaled the city walls here to defeat the Chinese. This, the city's northern gate, dates from the mid-6th century and was rebuilt in 1714. In ancient legend, the gate's namesake, Hyonmu, was a guardian of the north.

Hyonmu Gate

60 • Choesung Pavilion

Sitting on Moran Hill's highest point, Choesung Pavilion offers a scenic view. It was built in the mid-6th century, moving to its current location in 1716. The pavilion was used as an army command headquarters during ancient battles.

61 • Kim Il Sung Stadium

Here stood the athletic field where Kim made his famous homecoming speech (see "Kaeson Revolutionary Site," below). Moranbong Stadium was built on the site in 1954. It was enlarged in 1982 and rechristened "Kim Il Sung Stadium." Seating 100,000, the stadium hosts sports events and political rallies. It is also one of the main venues for the synchronized gymnastics show known as "mass games."

■ MASS GAMES

On a clear summer day, in the stands of Kim Il Sung Stadium, a crowd of 10,000 schoolchildren proclaims its loyalty to the Communist Party. As a throng of their classmates goose-step in colorful uniforms across the playing field, the students, all holding lettered cards, flash a slogan: "SOCIALIST REVOLUTION!" the cards read. The students flash a colorful representation of a Korean flag. And then, in a perfectly syn-

Kim Il Sung Stadium

Mass games performance

chronized move: "LONG LIVE THE GREAT LEADER KIM IL SUNG!"

This is how Urban Lehner of the *Wall Street Journal* describes a 1989 performance of mass games. Lehner aptly defines mass games as "combination halftime shows and propaganda pep rallies." Gymnasts perform coordinated displays on the field, while behind them, flashcards are held up in the stands to form huge mosaic-like images. A single event can involve as many as 50,000 participants.

The regime alleges that Kim Il Sung developed mass games in the 1930s, during his guerrilla war against the Japanese. In fact, the country's first mass games were held in 1946 (with a modest 30 gymnasts) and were almost certainly inspired by the Soviets.

In his analysis of mass gymnastic displays, Petr Roubal identifies their four core values. *Strength* – projected in martial imagery and athletic physiques – represents the nation's military might. *Discipline* parallels the leadership's control over its people: top-down organization to achieve a collective goal. *Beauty* radiates from the human body and its synchronized movements. The performers' *youth* casts the regime as brimming with energy and potential.

Mass games are used as ideological training, to inculcate young people with a collective spirit. The games also serve as a show of loyalty to the Kims and a means of dazzling visiting foreign leaders.

62 • Kaeson Revolutionary Site

Unveiled in 1987, this site commemorates the historic rally on October 14, 1945, when thousands welcomed Kim Il Sung home after liberation.

The regime claims Kim was being feted for having liberated Korea. Not so: this Soviet-sponsored rally celebrated liberation *by the Soviets*, a fact Kim himself acknowledged in his speech. Nevertheless, in the mural depicting the event (see photo, pages 156-157) – and even in official photos – the Soviet officers who stood behind Kim on the podium have been airbrushed out.

At this rally the population got its first glimpse of Kim, who had been known only by reports of his partisan deeds. The crowd was reportedly disappointed by his youth and lack of charisma. (Rumors even circulated that this Kim was an impostor – a story that lingered in South Korea for decades.)

Beside the mural, a stone-slab monument summarizes Kim's remarks. Kim told his listeners the time had come to build a new Korea. "Let those with strength give strength," he urged; "let those with knowledge give knowledge; let those with money give money."

63 • Arch of Triumph

This monument immortalizes Kim's guerrilla war against the Japanese. Kim supposedly launched his partisan campaign in 1925, at the tender age of 13. In 1945 Kim returned to Pyongyang and delivered a victory speech nearby (see "Kaeson Revolutionary Site," above).

At the top of the arch are inscribed the words to the "Song of General Kim Il Sung." The reliefs below represent the guerrilla war and socialist construction – the twin pillars of North Korean agitprop.

At 60 meters tall, this triumphal arch is the world's largest. As North Koreans like to point out, it surpasses even the Arc de Triomphe in Paris. The comparison is no coincidence. From the flagwaving relief figures to the rosette ornaments, this monument has borrowed much from its French predeces-

< Arch of Triumph

sor. (In turn, the Arc de Triomphe draws from the triumphal arches of imperial Rome.) But the three-tiered roof gives a nod to Korean national architecture.

64 • Arch of Triumph Square

The government offices on this square, built in 1954, were among the many buildings constructed by Chinese soldiers. To recognize China's crucial assistance during and after the Korean War, the regime christened this "Mao Zedong Square." But it was later renamed. Why was this homage to Mao revoked? Perhaps the regime was symbolically asserting its independence amidst the Sino-Soviet dispute. Or perhaps the escalating cult of Kim Il Sung left no room for tributes to foreign leaders.

65 • Ryonghwa Temple

Built in the 1920s, this temple is one of the few in Pyongyang where worship is still permitted. Ryonghwa was the temple most frequented by foreign Buddhist visitors before Kwangbop Temple was rebuilt. The regime maintains that 10,000 Buddhists are still practicing nationwide.

66 • Yongmyong Temple

Vanished site.
Yongmyong Temple once ranked as one of Pyongyang's major historic sites. It consisted of eight houses of worship, only one of which survived the Sino-Japanese War. The remaining building was then destroyed in the Korean War. Today, among the temple ruins, an eight-story granite pagoda remains standing. Even the regime acknowledges Yongmyong's importance – but has not rebuilt it.

Mao Zedong Square (today Arch of Triumph Square)

Ryonghwa Temple

67 • Friendship Tower

The Friendship Tower honors the Chinese People's Volunteers sent into the Korean War to rescue the North. The tower was unveiled in 1959, the year after Chinese forces withdrew. Fittingly, it was built near the Chinese Embassy; tourists from China routinely come here to lay flowers.

The tower's inscription hails Chinese assistance, and Korean-Chinese friendship, as "immortal." Inside the tower is a memorial hall. Three murals depict Chinese soldiers fighting alongside the Korean People's Army and helping rebuild the country. And two books list the names of 308 Chinese officers who fell in battle.

In 1984 the tower was rebuilt and enlarged to 30 meters tall, precisely as high as the Liberation Tower honoring the Soviets. With such evenhandedness the regime wished to stake out an equidistance between its two patrons. The difference is that the name "Friendship Tower" does not even hint at the nation's debt to China. But then, North Korea never looked up to China as it did to the Soviet Union.

■ THE CHINESE INTERVENTION

The envoys arrived quietly, but the note they carried spoke volumes. On the night of October 8, 1950, two Chinese diplomats entered a bunker deep beneath Moran Hill. They bore a

**Peng Dehuai
and
Kim Il Sung**

1953

crucial message for Kim Il Sung.

The diplomats found Kim quarreling over defense with Vice Premier Pak Hon Yong. Kim insisted it was time to retreat to the mountains and wage a guerrilla war. With UN troops closing in, the nation's fate hung in the balance.

Timidly, the diplomats waited until the shouting was over and Pak left. Only then did Kim acknowledge their presence. One of them, Chinese ambassador Ni Ziliang, handed Kim a telegram from Mao. The Chinese leader had approved Kim's request and was sending troops to defend North Korea.

Kim was elated by his good fortune. "How wonderful!" he exclaimed. "How wonderful!" Passing around shots of whisky, he proposed a toast to victory.

The Chinese entered the Korean War as quietly as Ambassador Ni delivered his message. On October 14, the first of hundreds of thousands of troops slipped across the Yalu River, unannounced and undetected. Only after China's general attack on October 25 did UN forces realize who was facing them across the front lines.

Mao had reason to tread lightly. He feared an all-out war

< Friendship Tower

with the United States. For the same reason, China maintained the fiction that its troops were "volunteers."

Yet the self-effacing Chinese played a pivotal role. Their counteroffensive hurled UN forces back across the 38th parallel, saving North Korea from oblivion. The crusade claimed 150,000 Chinese lives.

China's intervention led to frictions between the two countries' leaderships. Commander Peng Dehuai alienated Kim by usurping control of the war and treating him as a subordinate. North Korea, for its part, sometimes downplayed the Chinese contribution.

Despite the tensions at the top, Chinese soldiers won over the local population with their helpfulness and scrupulous conduct. Postwar cooperation further strengthened the amity. Trading in their rifles for picks and shovels, Chinese troops helped rebuild the country's houses, bridges and dams. Grateful North Koreans gave the People's Volunteers a warm sendoff at Pyongyang Railway Station when they withdrew in October 1958.

68 • Television tower

The television age dawned in Korea in 1961, when South Korea made its first regular broadcasts. Not to be outdone, Kim Il Sung ordered the creation of a North Korean television industry. The North made its first broadcasts in 1963. And it began broadcasting in color in 1974 – six years before South Korea.

Broadcasting range in Pyongyang remained limited until around 1967, when this television tower was completed. The concrete spire soars almost 200 meters over Moran Hill. Halfway up the tower is an observation deck. Southwest of the tower stands the Central Broadcasting Station.

Television tower

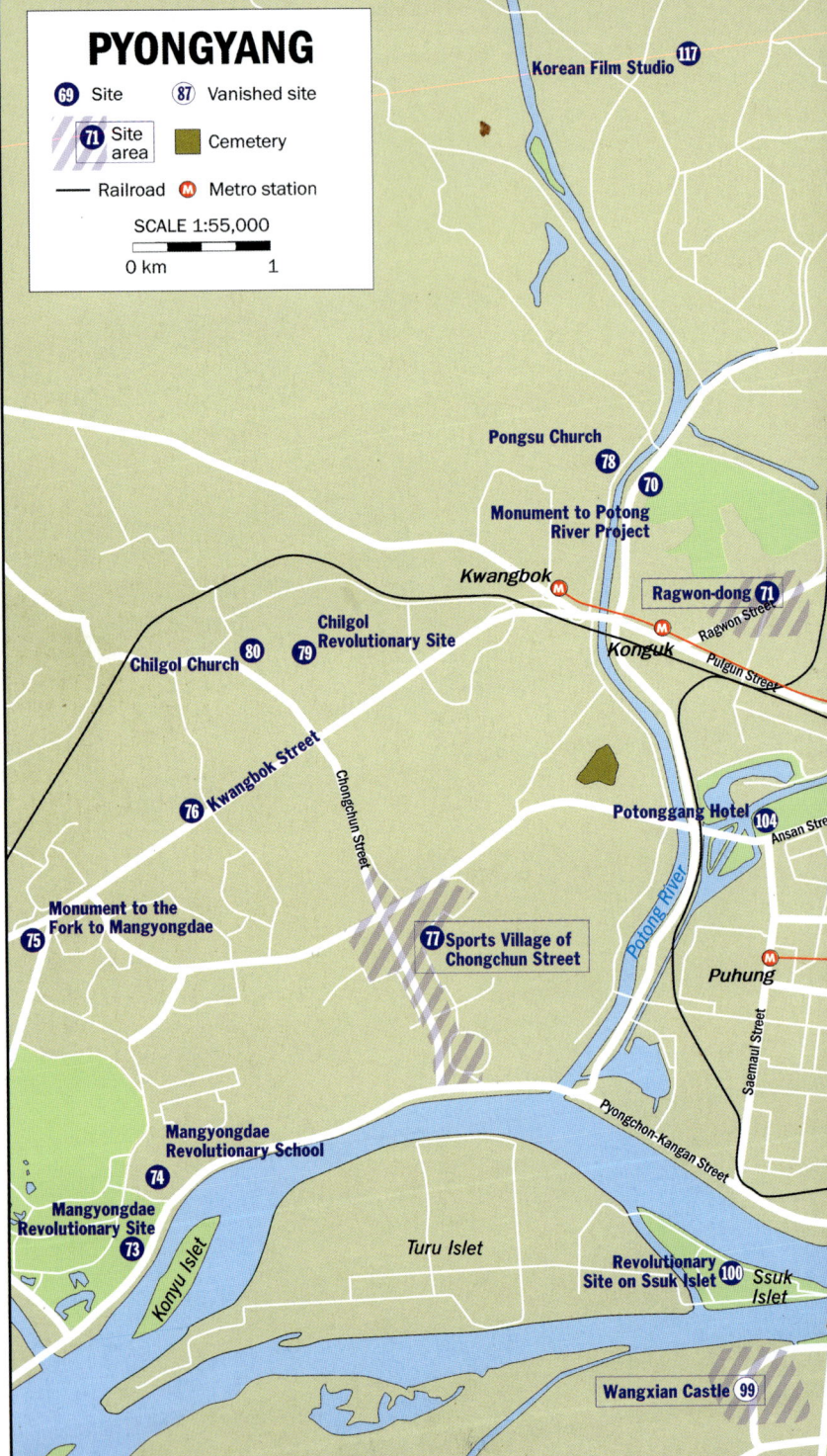

PYONGYANG

- **69** Site
- **87** Vanished site
- **71** Site area
- Cemetery
- — Railroad
- **M** Metro station

SCALE 1:55,000

0 km   1

Korean Film Studio **117**

Pongsu Church **78**
70

Monument to Potong
River Project

Kwangbok **M**
Ragwon-dong **71**
Ragwon Street

Konguk
Pulgun Street

Chilgol
Revolutionary Site
80 **79**
Chilgol Church

Kwangbok Street **76**

Chongchun Street

Monument to the
Fork to Mangyongdae
75

Potonggang Hotel **104**
Ansan Street

Potong River

77 Sports Village of
Chongchun Street

Puhung **M**

Saemaul Street

Mangyongdae
Revolutionary School
74

Mangyongdae
Revolutionary Site
73

Konyu Islet

Turu Islet

Pyongchon-Kangan Street

Revolutionary
Site on Ssuk Islet **100** *Ssuk Islet*

Wangxian Castle **99**

Elsewhere in Pyongyang

Potonggang District

69 • Ryugyong Hotel

A giant among giants, the 105-story Ryugyong Hotel bestrides the city like a colossus. At 323 meters, it stands as tall as the Eiffel Tower and ranks among the 20 tallest buildings in the world. The finished hotel is to contain 3,000 rooms and to be topped by three revolving restaurants with a view all the way to the west coast.

However, no one knows if the Ryugyong will ever be completed. It was intended to open in June 1989 for the World Festival of Youth and Students. But only the shell of the building was finished when construction was halted. Foreign accounts blame the work stoppage on crooked elevator shafts, cracking concrete or simply a lack of funds. To this day, the building sits empty.

With its monumental scale and turret-like projections, the Ryugyong faintly echoes Moscow's Stalinist skyscrapers. And its pyramid silhouette speaks to the regime's pharaonic ambitions. Such grandiosity is nothing new. What astonishes is the building's intended function. A hotel, in a country that straitjackets all travel? Why would this hyper-isolationist regime construct its biggest building for foreign visitors?

Oneupmanship was a key motive. A South Korean firm had just finished construction of what was then the world's tallest hotel, the Stamford in Singapore. The same regime that claims to "envy nothing in the world" wanted to steal the South Koreans' thunder.

Ironically, the only recognition the Ryugyong has earned has been the scorn of foreign journalists. They equate the project with the North Korean economy: overreaching and stalled.

Sojang Hill, where the Ryugyong stands, was previously a children's park, and before that, a graveyard. (One wonders: Were the graves moved?)

70 • Monument to the Potong River Improvement Project

Periodic floods have long plagued Pyongyang. To prevent flood-

< Ryugyong Hotel

ing and improve irrigation, the Japanese launched a project to reroute the Potong River. After liberation, the Communists completed the job in a mere 55 days. The meandering Potong was redirected straight into the Taedong, and its original riverbed was converted into a canal. On both sides of the canal, protected by levees, arose the Potonggang Pleasure Park.

The North Koreans hailed their achievement, in Stalinist phraseology, as "the remaking of nature." Ironically, nature responded in kind: in July 1946, around the time the project was completed, floods once again inundated Pyongyang.

The monument was put up in 1971, on the 25th anniversary of the project's groundbreaking. This 13-meter-tall stone tower stands on Ponghwa Hill.

■ THE 1967 FLOOD

News of natural disasters in North Korea is often hushed up by the regime. Thus the outside world learned little about Pyongyang's disastrous 1967 flood. However, a foreign witness to the disaster has provided the following information:

Heavy August rains caused the Taedong River to swell. When this torrent met the incoming tides from the Yellow Sea, disaster struck. The river burst its banks and inundated most of central Pyongyang. The flood swept through at night, taking the city by surprise. Kim Il Sung Square was buried under several meters of mud, and fuel tanks at the railway sta-

Mangyongdae Revolutionary Site

tion were tossed about until they erupted into sheets of flame. Enormous casualties resulted, especially among the many in East Pyongyang who still lived in single-story dwellings.

71 • Ragwon-dong

Behind the name "Ragwon" ("Paradise") lies a neighborhood that has historically endured hardship and neglect. Under the Japanese, this was a slum area full of mud huts. Not until the early 1960s did major housing construction begin. Ragwon Street, the neighborhood's main thoroughfare, was completed in 1975. The apartments in its pastel-hued tower blocks average a relatively small 70 sq. meters.

West of Ragwon-dong, near Palgol Bridge, lies a cluster of Western-style villas, guarded and fenced off. Could these be guest houses for foreign residents?

72 • Monument to the Victorious Fatherland Liberation War

The regime unveiled this monument in 1993 for the 40th anniversary of the Korean War armistice. Ten sculpture groups face one another across a vast plaza. Each depicts a different set of Northern combatants. One portrays People's Army soldiers welcomed by civilians as they "liberate" South Korea. Another honors the defenders of Height 1211 (known in the West as "Heartbreak Ridge"). At the far end of the plaza stands a sculpture entitled *Victory*: a bronze soldier raises a flag and cheers. Compare this triumphalism with the war-is-hell realism of the Korean War Memorial in Washington, D.C., and the question arises: who won the war?

Mangyongdae District

Mangyongdae is best known as Kim Il Sung's native village. As a result, it became sacred ground. But that did not prevent officials from clearing the wooded hills and planting them with orchards. In 1970 an angry Kim ordered a halt to the intrusion.

73 • Mangyongdae Revolutionary Site

Official lore has it that Kim Il Sung was born at Mangyongdae. That myth is debunked by an unlikely source: Kim's own memoirs. Kim writes that his mother went to her home village,

Students of Mangyongdae Revolutionary School

Chilgol, to give birth (see "Chilgol Revolutionary Site," page 104). Kim called Mangyongdae his "birthplace" only because it was his father's ancestral home, and Kim's childhood home.

The small thatched-roof house at Mangyongdae is a national shrine. Ever since it was designated a historical site in 1947, North Koreans have been brought here to pay tribute. Legends have been woven around various spots of the village, like the "warship rock" where Kim and his playmates pretended to fight the Japanese. Every nursery in the country contains a model of the village to teach children these saccharine stories.

The presentation at Mangyongdae plays up the Great Leader's humble origins. Visitors are routinely shown the lopsided clay jar that was the best the family could afford. But the poverty fails to register amid the manicured lawns and the endless procession of Koreans visiting in their finest dress.

The Mangyongdae Revolutionary Museum, founded in 1970, displays Kim's childhood possessions and glorifies his "revolutionary" family. His parents and paternal grandparents are buried nearby. Kim's great-grandfather, Kim Ung U, worked as a caretaker of landlords' graves in Mangyongdae, but those graves have since vanished.

74 • Mangyongdae Revolutionary School

Mangyongdae Revolutionary School was founded in 1947 to educate children of dead "revolutionaries" (anti-Japanese guerrillas and, later, Korean War soldiers). Today, the school simply serves the children of high Party officials, not just orphans. Even students with families leave them behind and are raised collectively at this boarding school.

Run by the Armed Forces Ministry, the school places its all-male studentry under military regimentation, complete with army uniforms and training. These janissaries are nurtured as the country's future elite. Even Kim Jong Il attended the school (but not in Pyongyang – the institution moved north for the duration of the Korean War).

North of here, unmarked on official maps, lies Kim Il Sung Military University. (Could this be where promising graduates of the Revolutionary School continue their studies?) Here once stood a Presbyterian church where Kim Il Sung's mother worshipped.

75 • Monument to the Fork to Mangyongdae

This stone monument marks "the road not taken," based on the following anecdote:

After liberation in 1945, Kim Il Sung returned to Pyongyang for the first time in 20 years. Traveling to Kangson to meet with factory workers, Kim passed by Mangyongdae, where his grandparents, aunt and uncle still lived. For a minute he stopped the car beside the fork in the road. Then – putting his political duties before his family reunion – he ordered the car to keep going.

Kim finally returned home to Mangyongdae five days later, on the evening of October 14, after his historic speech in Pyongyang.

76 • Kwangbok Street

Kwangbok Street, completed in 1988, was the most ambitious housing project North Korea had ever undertaken. An unprecedented 260 tower blocks were built, containing more than 25,000 apartments.

Residents of dilapidated 1950s housing were relocated here, to the city's outskirts, in order to ease "overcrowding." Overcrowding, in a city that feels so empty? In fact, the population is dispersed throughout Pyongyang for civil-defense reasons. The regime has gone so far as to order mass deportations from the city – starting, of course, with the politically unreliable.

Despite Pyongyang's light traffic, Kwangbok and other streets were built wide, with five or six lanes in each direction. This too likely stems from defense concerns – to allow rapid evacuations and/or the movement of armored columns.

77 • Sports Village of Chongchun Street

Officially, the Sports Village was constructed for the 1989 World Festival of Youth and Students. In truth, the authorities had a more ambitious purpose in mind: to co-host the 1988 Olympics. But North Korea's Olympic bid foundered. In the end, only the World Festival – a recurring communist-bloc event – came to Pyongyang. With a reported 15,000 participants, it was the biggest international event ever held in North Korea.

The Sports Village contains nine gymnasiums, each for a different sport, plus an indoor swimming pool. Each gymnasium seats between 2,000 and 5,000 people.

■ PYONGYANG'S OLYMPIC DEFEAT

When Seoul was selected to host the 1988 Olympics, North Korea's reaction was most unsportsmanlike. Resentful of South Korea's higher international profile, the regime blasted

Kwangbok Street

Sports Village of Chongchun Street

the choice as a "criminal act" and campaigned for an international boycott.

Then the regime changed tack. In 1984, with Seoul's preparations already well underway, North Korea suddenly demanded to co-host the Olympics. South Korea's conciliatory counter-offer – for Pyongyang to host a couple of sports – was summarily rejected.

Many questioned the North's intentions. Richard Pound of the International Olympic Committee says the regime was "so outrageous in its demands and so intransigent in its negotiations" that its Olympic bid seemed insincere. Indeed, its very purpose may have been to throw a wrench into the South's plans. To this end the regime stopped at nothing: A South Korean passenger plane was blown up in 1987, and the bomber, a North Korean agent, confessed that her objective was to scare visitors away from the Olympics.

In the end, only a handful of countries joined the boycott, and the regime failed either to halt the Olympics or to muscle its way in. But in the meantime, it had built stadiums and hotels for the never-to-be "Pyongyang-Seoul Olympics."

78 • Pongsu Church

Along with the Catholic Changchung Cathedral, the Protestant Pongsu Church opened in 1988, just in time for the World

Festival of Youth and Students. Some observers suggest the churches were built merely to serve foreign worshippers and foster the illusion of religious freedom. So are services simply staged? The jury is still out. Some foreigners, showing up unexpectedly for 10 a.m. Sunday services, have found the churches closed. Others say services were proceeding as scheduled.

Regardless, these churches do serve political ends. Through them the regime can seek support from Korean Christians abroad for its policies on reunification. Visiting South Koreans have described the sermons at Pongsu as political speeches, devoid of religious content. The churches are also used to attract aid from abroad. For instance, the Presbyterian Church (U.S.A.) bankrolls Pongsu's noodle factory, which feeds some of the country's undernourished.

79 • Chilgol Revolutionary Site

The regime calls Kang Ban Sok the "mother of Korea." Her main achievement was to give birth to Kim Il Sung. Her home village, Chilgol, became a revolutionary site in the early 1970s, when Kim extended his personality cult to his family. Kang's statue stands on the grounds.

Changdok School, which Kim attended from 1923 to 1925,

Pongsu Church

Changdok School, Chilgol

features a bronze statue of Kim as a schoolboy. Reverently displayed are relics like Kim's schooldesk. Kim's maternal grandfather, Kang Don Uk, is honored here with a monument. He is credited with founding Changdok School. In fact, it was established by American missionary Samuel A. Moffett (see "Yangchon," page 48).

80 • Chilgol Church

The man who eradicated religion in North Korea had a devout Christian mother. Official lore does not admit it, but the Protestant Chilgol Church, built in 1992, is said to be a reconstruction of the church Kim Il Sung's mother attended. As a boy, Kim sometimes accompanied her to services. But, as he once recalled, he was bored and wished he had gone fishing instead.

Taesong District

Sites on Mount Taesong are covered separately, in a later chapter.

81 • Kumgang Temple

Kumgang is arguably Pyongyang's most significant Buddhist temple. It is prized as an outstanding example of Koguryo architecture. The temple was built in 498 but disappeared after the 11th century. Its ruins were not fully uncovered until 1938. Later discoveries of earthen walls spelled the end for plans to locate the Kim Il Sung University campus near here.

In 1998 the temple and its pagoda were reconstructed. The rebuilt pagoda stands seven stories and 70 meters high.

82 • Kim Il Sung University

This, the state's first university, was inaugurated in 1946. It was originally called the "North Korean People's University." Its first president, Kim Tu-bong, was a distinguished politician who was later purged by Kim Il Sung.

This university is the country's biggest and most prestigious, with 14 departments and 12,000 students. The main building, built in 1948, is a rare surviving example of architecture under Soviet rule. Building No. 2, rising 22 stories, was once the tallest in the country.

In 1960, after the admissions department's inevitable decision, Kim Jong Il enrolled at the university named for his father. Kim graduated in 1964 with a degree in political economics. On view here are personal effects from his school days. An oversized picture shows him on kitchen duty at military camp (see "Oun Revolutionary Site," page 142); the ladle he used is reverently displayed.

Kim Il Sung's scribes earnestly assert that when he died, flocks of rare birds visited his campus statue, "expressing condolences."

83 • Kumsusan Memorial Palace

This four-story mansion, inaugurated in 1976 as "Kumsusan Assembly Hall," was Kim Il Sung's official residence. Henry

Kim Il Sung University

Kumsusan Memorial Palace

Scott Stokes of the *New York Times* described it as "a long, gray building with a great moat, square turrets, mock Versailles gates and a crenelated central tower." Why was a militant communist living in such an opulent mansion? According to official lore, the people gave it to Kim "to alleviate the pain of the great leader."

Kim's body lay in state here after his death in 1994. Soon afterward, the regime decided to turn the building into a mausoleum. Its windows were bricked up, its interior renovated. Renamed "Kumsusan Memorial Palace," it was unveiled one year after Kim's death.

Strictly off-limits during Kim's lifetime, the palace is a site of mass pilgrimage today. (Few foreigners, however, are allowed to visit this holy of holies.) The front lawn has been turned into a nearly 100,000 sq. meter plaza. Moving sidewalks ferry visitors down a covered walkway 1 kilometer long.

Inside the palace, air jets and shoe washers remove every speck of dust from visitors. They are led up an escalator and through a hall dominated by a statue of Kim. Finally, on the top floor of the palace, recumbent in a glass coffin, is the Great Leader. A red flag (the Party banner?) lies draped across his body. Visitors circle the coffin and bow to Kim on all four sides.

Any resemblance to Lenin or Mao's displayed remains is

entirely intentional. Indeed, advice on embalming was sought from the curators of Lenin's Tomb.

Kumsusan was only one of Kim's many palaces. The largest of these, say South Korean sources, is the Mount Chamo Villa of Longevity in Pyongsung (north of Pyongyang). This villa was allegedly linked with Kumsusan via a secret tunnel or metro line.

84 • Tower of Immortality

Slender stone towers sprouted up across the country after the death of Kim Il Sung. They all bear the same slogan: "The Great Leader Comrade Kim Il Sung Will Always Be with Us." The regime says these towers inspire citizens to "pray for the immortality" of Kim – curious phrasing for an atheist state.

The most prominent Tower of Immortality – 92 meters tall – stands at the approach to Kumsusan Memorial Palace. Traffic flows underneath the tower's arched base. It was completed in 1997, on the third anniversary of Kim's death.

East Pyongyang

Historically a second-rate industrial suburb, East Pyongyang has long played Newark to West Pyongyang's Manhattan. The ravages of the Korean War hit it early. And postwar reconstruction arrived late. For many years, East Pyongyang consisted mainly of factories and poor one-story houses. Some industry still remains here (particularly in Songyo District).

85 • Tower of the Juche Idea

This ribbed obelisk honors Kim Il Sung's doctrine of *juche* (national self-reliance). Kim first mentioned *juche* in 1955, while criticizing the imitation of Soviet practices. Kim said Koreans had to stop taking cues from foreign powers and start believing in their own abilities. Over time the regime spun this simple credo into a woolly ideology. *Juche* replaced Marxism-Leninism as the ideological underpinning for Kim's dictatorship.

The Tower of the Juche Idea was one of the architectural trophies unveiled for Kim's 70th birthday in 1982. It is clad with 25,550 slabs of white granite, one for each day of Kim's life (leap years must have been overlooked). The tower rises 170 meters, surpassing the Washington Monument by one meter (just to show who was *really* Father of His Country).

< Tower of the Juche Idea

An alcove at the tower's base is studded with stone plaques from *juche* study groups around the world. (Exactly how the regime organized these overseas fan clubs bears further investigation.) An elevator carries visitors up to an outdoor observation deck 150 meters high. Topping the monument is a stained-glass red flame wired to flicker at night.

In front of the tower stand gargantuan bronze figures of a worker, a peasant and an intellectual. Above their heads, they hold, respectively, a hammer, a sickle and a writing brush, composing the emblem of the Korean Workers' Party. Sculpture groups on either side depict the fruits of *juche* in fields such as industry, public health, and agriculture.

The tower's riverside locale was once home to the Industrial and Agricultural Exhibition.

86 • Pyongyang Maternity Hospital

This hospital for expectant mothers was inaugurated in 1980, after nine months' gestation. The curved wings of the building symbolize a mother cradling her baby.

Noting the eerie stillness, foreign journalists dismiss this as a "Potemkin hospital." But Norbert Vollertsen, a German doctor who once practiced in Pyongyang, demurs. It is a real hospital, he says, albeit one set aside for the elite.

The hospital teems with high-tech equipment, including closed-circuit cameras for fathers to see their babies. Fathers are kept quarantined from the newborns for several days, for fear of germs. Ironically, the same restrictions do not apply to foreigners touring the hospital.

87 • Pyongyang Airport

Vanished site.

On June 29, 1950, as dusk settled over Pyongyang Airport, the drone of American B-26 planes filled the skies. They bombed and destroyed the aircraft on the tarmac – the opening salvo in a three-year air war against the North.

In October the Americans captured Pyongyang and took over the airport. General MacArthur reviewed his troops here amid high spirits. The GIs felt sure they would be home by Christmas.

But as Chinese forces advanced, the Americans were forced to retreat. Everything they could not haul away from the airport was torched: food, ammunition, winter clothing. Then the airport itself was burned to the ground. Plumes of black

Pyongyang Maternity Hospital

smoke above the city marked the Americans' scorched-earth policy at its merciless climax.

After the war this airport was abandoned in favor of Sunan Airport. Like Youido Plaza in Seoul, another former military airstrip, the one-time Pyongyang Airport is now largely consumed by urban sprawl.

88 • Pyongyang Downtown Airfield

Vanished site.

Like so many conflicts, the Korean War inspired remarkable improvisation. In 1951, with Pyongyang Airport under constant attack, the resourceful North Koreans transformed a nearby boulevard into a makeshift landing strip. They razed the buildings along the road and set up aircraft hangars on the side streets. But U.S. air reconnaissance caught on to the scheme. The Americans promptly bombed the runway into rubble.

Changchung Cathedral

89 • Changchung Cathedral

The regime alleges it has spent "vast funds" to rebuild churches destroyed in the Korean War. In fact, though Pyongyang once had dozens of churches, today it has only three. All of them lie far outside the city center and were built relatively recently.

Changchung Cathedral opened in 1988 – whether it is new, or a reconstruction of a prewar church, is unclear. What happens when an atheist regime runs a token Catholic church? For starters, Changchung has no resident priest; a proper Mass can only be held when foreign priests visit.

The noodle factory on the church premises was paid for in part by the Archdiocese of Seoul and Korean Catholics from America.

90 • Party Foundation Monument

To mark the 50th anniversary of the Korean Workers' Party, this monument was unveiled in 1995. Its three granite fists rise 50 meters into the air. They wield a hammer, sickle and writing brush – the three tools in the Party emblem. Encircling this is a wall with reliefs depicting the Party's history. They dubiously trace the Party's origins back to the "Down-with-Imperialism Union," supposedly founded by Kim Il Sung at the age of 14.

91 • Sama-dong

North Korea is one of a handful of countries that still carries out public executions. As crowds spew hatred, political prisoners and common criminals alike face a firing squad or a hangman's noose. The human-rights group Amnesty International reported one such execution in 1988 in the neighborhood of Sama-dong. (It may have occurred in East Pyongyang Stadium: such executions take place in stadiums or other open areas.) The regime denies holding public executions and claims that the death penalty is only rarely imposed.

92 • Munsu-dong

In the 1960s North Korea started courting Third World nations in a bid for increased diplomatic recognition. The fruits of that charm offensive can be seen in the collection of embassies in Munsu-dong. Around 1980 the regime turned this neighborhood into a diplomatic quarter and encouraged embassies to move here. (Several embassies of former communist-bloc states chose to remain in West Pyongyang.)

Party Foundation Monument

93 • Munsubong Revolutionary Site

No act of Kim Il Sung's, it seems, is too trivial to be revolutionary. This site commemorates Kim's planting of a larch tree on April 6, 1947, when this hillside was made into a park. April 6 was thereafter celebrated as Reforestation Day. Citizens were encouraged to follow the Great Leader's example and plant trees all over the country's hills and mountains.

Other sites

94 • May Day Stadium

With a capacity of 150,000, this stadium is the world's largest. (Seoul's Olympic Stadium, by comparison, seats 100,000.) Its undulating canopy is intended to resemble a magnolia. This stadium on Rungna Islet was built for Pyongyang's abortive Olympic bid. But in the end, it was used only for the 1989 World Festival of Youth and Students. The opening and closing ceremonies were held here.

It was then that the regime's penchant for tightly controlled pageantry collided with the presence of freethinking foreign youths. Danish and Swedish students unfurled unofficial banners in support of human-rights group Amnesty International and were beaten by security forces.

May Day Stadium

Taedong Bridge

95 • Taedong Bridge

Built in 1922, this iron frame bridge was probably the first to span the Taedong River. Taedong Bridge became an early casualty of the Korean War, as ROK and U.S. forces took the city. Racing through East Pyongyang, ROK General Paik Sun Yup had just reached the rotary near the bridgehead. "As our lead vehicles pulled into the intersection, an ear-splitting explosion came from the direction of the bridge, and chunks of flying iron filled the air," Paik writes in his memoirs. "The bridge's central span dropped neatly into the river." The North Korean People's Army had blown it up.

In December 1950, with Chinese and North Korean troops poised to recapture Pyongyang, fleeing civilians clambered across the bridge's half-submerged wreckage. This desperate crossing was captured in a Pulitzer-Prize-winning photo.

96 • Yanggak Bridge

The railway bridge here was blown up by retreating Communist forces during the Korean War. The Americans rebuilt the bridge with forced labor. But just when it was completed, they received orders to abandon the city and destroy the bridge. After the war the Chinese helped reconstruct the bridge. A bridge for car traffic was built beside it in 1986.

97 • Yanggakdo Hotel

Yanggakdo, opened in 1995, is the country's most luxurious hotel. Its swank recreation, including a nightclub and casino, seems the very antithesis of the mirthless city outside. Indeed, the hotel is strategically placed on an island, sequestering visitors from the rest of Pyongyang. Nevertheless, one senses that the state is never far away – perhaps its ears are concealed in the false walls hugging the outside of each room.

The hotel's Western-style comforts are an unintended gift from the French. Despite North Korea's abysmal credit rating, Roger-Patrice Pelat, a crony of French president Francois Mitterand, got his government to extend a loan for the hotel's construction. Predictably, North Korea defaulted on the loan and was left to finish the hotel on its own. All told, construction took almost 10 years.

98 • Tongil Street

Like Kwangbok Street (see page 101), Tongil Street is a suburban housing development built to ease "overpopulation" in Pyongyang. It encompasses 290 tower blocks, rising as high as 30 stories. The project was completed in 1993.

Outsiders often regard Pyongyang's rows of concrete tower blocks as Orwellian. They may be, but similar projects are also found in Seoul. In both Koreas, high-rises are a response to high population density.

This street is named Tongil ("Reunification") and sited at the city's southern gateway, expressing aspirations for unity with the South. A statue park underscores the theme. One sculpture depicts a Northern and a Southern girl running into each other's arms.

Construction work on the street has unearthed a slew of ancient artifacts. The regime maintains that this site was the 5000-year-old capital of the "Tangun Kingdom" (see "Tomb of King Tangun," page 143). In fact, the relics most likely come from the Lelang commandery (see "Wangxian Castle," below).

99 • Wangxian Castle

Vanished site.
The story of Wangxian Castle highlights the interplay between

Tongil Street under construction

archaeology and politics in North Korea. An ancient citadel, Wangxian stood amid 1,400 grave mounds scattered across today's Rangrang District. Japanese archaeologists who began work here in 1913 unearthed the remnants of an advanced civilization. Within the castle's mud walls lay streets surfaced with brick and lined with gutters. And the tombs yielded dazzling treasures: skillfully crafted mirrors and exquisite lacquer paintings.

Wangxian Castle was identified as the capital of Lelang ("Rangrang" in Korean), which extended across northwest Korea from 108 B.C.E. to 313 C.E. Most historians agree that Lelang was a commandery (military settlement) of the Chinese. The tombs are indeed in Chinese style and contain many objects imported from China. Ancient records appear to confirm Lelang's Chinese origins.

North Korean history books used to acknowledge the same. But today the regime concedes no foreign influences, even ancient ones. It now maintains the settlement was Korean and says all evidence to the contrary was fabricated by "reptile historians of the Japanese imperialists." Once one of the city's most visited sites, the tombs are no longer accessible to tourists, and apartment blocks have been built atop the castle site.

100 • Revolutionary Site on Ssuk Islet

On May 2, 1948, following the North-South Joint Conference, politicians from South Korea met here privately with Kim Il Sung. The parkland site features a hut on stilts and a ferry boat, plus the United Front Tower, a 13.5-meter-tall monument to the conference.

■ THE NORTH-SOUTH JOINT CONFERENCE

It was a border neither side wanted. Yet by 1948, Korea's "temporary" division along the 38th parallel looked more and more permanent. To rally opposition to separate elections in the South, Kim Il Sung held the North-South Joint Conference. Participants called for the withdrawal of foreign troops and the holding of all-Korea elections before the formation of any government. But the event was window dressing for Kim's bid to take over all of Korea. On May 1 – breaking a conference pledge – the North unilaterally adopted a constitution. Kim must have had some explaining to do when he met Southern politicians on Ssuk Islet the next day. Many of them came away disillusioned.

One such politician was Kim Ku. The regime once denounced this nationalist leader as a traitor, but it has since honored him by engraving his name on the United Front Tower. The

Monument to the sinking of the _General Sherman_

regime explains that he "worked for collaboration with communism, thus turning over a new leaf." At the conference he did indeed find some common ground with Kim Il Sung. But Kim Ku also loudly objected to the North's confiscation of private property and its fealty to the Soviet Union.

101 • Monument to the sinking of the *General Sherman*

This stone monument was unveiled in 1986, celebrating the sinking of the American ship *General Sherman* exactly 120 years earlier. Cannons from the U.S. "pirate ship" lie beside the monument. (The ship's other cannons are displayed at the Korean Revolution Museum and the Korean Central History Museum.)

There may be other monuments to this event. Official sources describe a "stone monument to the repulsion of invaders," dating from 1871. Other sources mention a memorial on Konyu Islet commemorating the ship's destruction.

■ THE SINKING OF THE *GENERAL SHERMAN*

The *General Sherman* incident testifies to the West's aggressive "opening" of Asia. This U.S. merchant ship sailed up the Taedong River in 1866, on a mission to force the isolationist Koreans to open trade. As crowds gathered along the shore, the crew opened fire on them. Thus, when the *General Sherman* ran aground, angry locals torched the ship and killed everyone aboard.

The incident is rightly remembered as an example of U.S. imperialism and Korean resistance. But in North Korea the tale grows taller with each telling. The *General Sherman* is accused of seeking to loot ancient royal tombs. It is also accused of having "shamelessly carried out espionage activities" (thus retrofitting this story with the later deeds of the *Pueblo*: see below). A role has even been written in for the indefatigable Kim family. Since the 1970s the regime has claimed that the attack was led by Kim Il Sung's great-grandfather Kim Ung U.

102 • U.S.S. *Pueblo*

Captured in 1968, this U.S. vessel is proudly displayed as a trophy of war. It is also a powerful testimony to the regime's brinkmanship. Shrapnel damage still scars the deck. And two of the tour guides on board are former navymen who took part in the ship's seizure.

Kept hidden for decades, the *Pueblo* re-emerged in 1995 in

Wonsan as a tourist attraction. In 1999 the ship was moved to Pyongyang. It had been sailed around South Korea, in international waters (risking re-seizure by the United States).

The regime organizes tours of the *Pueblo,* particularly for army servicemen, for purposes of "anti-U.S. education." To drive the point home, the *Pueblo* is moored at the site where the *General Sherman* was destroyed more than a century earlier (see above).

■ THE CAPTURE OF THE *PUEBLO*

No incident came closer to reigniting war in Korea than the capture of the U.S.S. *Pueblo.* Sailing east of Wonsan in 1968, the vessel was eavesdropping on local communications. It was surrounded and shelled by six North Korean warships, killing one American. Inadequately armed, the *Pueblo* surrendered without resistance.

The captured Americans were tortured into signing confessions that they had violated North Korean waters. But the prisoners managed to signal their defiance to the outside world. Posing for propaganda photos, they raised their middle fingers, explaining this gesture to their captors as the "Hawaiian Good Luck Sign."

The crew went free only after 11 months and a U.S. apol-

A capturer, and now docent, of the *Pueblo*

U.S.S. *Pueblo*

ogy. The released crewmen denied they had ever left international waters.

In capturing the ship, the regime scored a great symbolic victory – and took a breathtaking gamble. Seizing an American ship was an act so reckless that some historians suspect a blunder by low-level officers. Pyongyang braced itself for war, holding air-raid drills and mobilizing the army. But the United States – already bogged down in Vietnam – did not retaliate.

103 • Pyongchon Revolutionary Site

Exact location unknown.

In 1945 Kim Il Sung selected this as the site of the nation's first munitions factory. The choice is hailed as a "revolutionary exploit." In fact, it was pure common sense: a vast Japanese-built arsenal already stood here.

At that time, just after liberation, Kim saw developing the defense industry as "the most important issue of the state." Given the pressing tasks Kim faced, this assertion is revealing. Did he anticipate, even then, reunifying Korea by force? Arms production remains a key concern today, not only for defense but for sale abroad (see "125 Factory," page 141).

Kim and his wife Kim Jong Suk visited this factory in 1948 and 1949. Official lore describes them – and 7-year-old Kim Jong Il! – test-firing submachine guns here.

104 • Potonggang Hotel

Potonggang Hotel is owned by the Unification Church, a messianic sect. Church leader Rev. Sun Myung Moon insisted that Potonggang have access to satellite TV. As a result, it is the only hotel in the country to receive CNN and other satellite channels. The hotel is run by Japanese followers of the sect and caters to foreigners. The Unification Church reportedly intends to open an interfaith center nearby.

■ THE REVEREND MOON

This charismatic Korean has cultivated his own cult of personality, calls himself the "true father" of all humanity and claims to be the key to his country's reunification. A member of the Kim dynasty? No, the Rev. Sun Myung Moon.

Moon, the founder of the Unification Church, was the unlikeliest of partners for the regime. A native of North Korea, he was imprisoned for "disturbing the social order" with his messianic preaching until, in 1950, he escaped and fled to the South. The experience made Moon a fervent anti-communist, who denounced Kim Il Sung as a creature of Satan.

But Moon's interest in reunification spurred him to seek a meeting with Kim. And his vast business empire, including the daily *Washington Times*, gave him the requisite clout. The two men's talks in Pyongyang in December 1991 cleared the way for the Unification Church to purchase Potonggang Hotel. Imagining these two rival messiahs facing off in negotiations reels the mind.

105 • Pyongyang Metro

The Pyongyang Metro owes an unmistakable architectural debt to its Moscow counterpart. Its stations are decked out with gleaming marble surfaces, chandeliers, and carved pillars, embracing Stalin's vision of the metro as a palace for the masses.

Also like the Moscow Metro, the Pyongyang Metro doubles as an air-raid shelter. It lies nearly 100 meters underground. At the foot of the escalators sit steel doors that can seal off the tunnels. Civil-defense planning may well have spurred the very creation of the metro, just as it prompted the construction of numerous tunnels and bunkers after the Korean War.

While the blueprints were copied from the Soviets, material and technical support came from the Chinese. China even delayed the Beijing metro project for two years in order to provide this help. Yet the regime has been too proud to acknowledge Chinese assistance.

Murals in each station illustrate the country's liberation and socialist construction. Such themes recur in the agitprop station names: "War Victory," "Nation-Building." This may be the only metro in the world whose stations are not named for orientation.

Pyongyang and Seoul acted out old rivalries as they built their respective metros. Pyongyang inaugurated its metro in 1973, a year ahead of Seoul. But Seoul now boasts eight metro lines, compared with Pyongyang's two. New lines serving East Pyongyang and Mangyongdae were scheduled to open in 2000 but have not been completed. Rumor has it that the metro was to cross the Taedong from the very start but that a cross-river tunnel collapsed during construction in 1971.

Located near the metro junction is the Underground Revolution Museum. In this recounting of the metro's construction, Kim Il Sung takes a starring role. One of the prized relics is the chair he sat in while watching the metro being built.

For more information, see www.pyongyang-metro.com, an unofficial website.

The Pyongyang Metro has the following stations:
Chollima Line (north-south) – opened 1973
- **Pulgunbyol** (Red Star)
  Theme: Advancing the revolutionary cause. Decorations: Sculptures of a worker and a soldier, representing the economic and defense fronts.
- **Chonu** (Comrades-in-Arms)
  Theme: The struggle for liberation.
- **Kaeson** (Triumphant Return)
  Theme: Kim's 1945 return to Pyongyang (the stop lies near the site of his return speech). Decorations: Mosaics of Kim's

speech, people welcoming democratic reforms, and the building of a new Korea.

- **Tongil** (Reunification)
  Theme: Korean reunification. Decorations: Lamps shaped like rainbow bridges; reliefs showing the people's hopes for unification.
- **Sungri** (Victory)
  Theme: North Korea as a people's paradise. Decorations: Mosaic of Pyongyang.
- **Ponghwa** (Torch)
  Theme: The struggle for liberation.
- **Yonggwang** (Glory)
  Theme: Victory celebrations at the end of the Korean War. Decorations: Mosaics of the skyline along the Taedong River; Lake Chon; Mount Paektu. Chandeliers shaped like fireworks; pillars shaped like torches.
- **Puhung** (Revival)
  Theme: Socialist innovation (industrial and agricultural). Decorations: Mosaic of Kim among the workers.

Hyoksin Line (west-east) – opened 1978
- **Kwangbok** (Rebirth)
  Theme: struggle of the anti-Japanese guerrillas. Decorations: Mural of the secret camp on Mount Paektu; mural of Lake Samji; reliefs of guerrillas studying the *juche* idea.
- **Konguk** (Nation-Building)
  Theme: achievements in building the country. Decorations: Mosaic of the skyline along the Potong River.
- **Hwanggumbol** (Golden Fields)
  Theme: Bumper crops produced by socialism. Decorations: Mosaics and murals of rice, wheat and corn on a cooperative farm. Reliefs of farm produce. Lamps shaped like grapes.
- **Konsol** (Construction)
  Theme: postwar reconstruction. Decorations: Murals of a blast furnace, of the rebuilding of Pyongyang, and of peasants going to cooperative farms.
- **Hyoksin** (Innovation)
  Theme: Socialist construction. Decorations: Murals of people announcing a shock-labor campaign.
- **Chonsung** (War Victory)
  Theme: The Korean War. Decorations: Mural of Kim Il Sung

Yonggwang Station, Pyongyang Metro

with army officers, celebrating victory.

- **Samhung** (Threefold Revival)
  Theme: Intellectual, moral and physical education (the stop lies near Kim Il Sung University). Decorations: Pictures of students of various ages studying.
- **Kwangmyong** (Light)
  Decorations: Murals of fruit and grain harvests.
  (This metro stop, near Kumsusan Memorial Palace, does not appear on North Korean maps and is apparently off-limits to the public. Some observers believe this metro stop may connect the palace with a secret bunker under Mount Taesong. Such an arrangement recalls the private metro line that Stalin ordered built from central Moscow to his dacha.)
- **Ragwon** (Paradise)
  Theme: Political and ideological unity; consolidating the revolution and constructing a socialist state. Decorations: Reliefs of deer and tigers (the stop is near the Central Zoo); a mural of a factory.

Note: The two metro lines meet at Chonu and Chonsung stations. The two stations routinely shown to visitors are the impressive Yonggwang and Puhung.

106 • Pyongyang walls

Vanished site. Not shown on map.
The Koguryo kingdom started erecting defensive walls around
Pyongyang in 552. This massive undertaking took 42 years to
finish. The city walls stretched 23 kilometers around what is
now Central and Pyongchon Districts. The walled city consisted
of four forts – northern, inner, central, and outer. The walls
gradually disappeared, though some stood until the early 20th
century. A few remnants remain on Moran Hill and the banks
of the Taedong River. Of the walled city's 16 original gates, five
survive: Taedong, Potong, Hyonmu, Chilsong, and Chongum.

107 • Chonsung Revolutionary Museum

Here is the complex where the leadership weathered the dark
hours of the Korean War. In what was an old quarry, Kim Il
Sung established his Supreme Headquarters.

Aboveground is the study room where Kim planned the
country's reconstruction. Displayed is the 1951 plan for rebuilding Pyongyang. Here too is the conference room where
Kim approved the armistice. Underground is the bunker where
he convened government and military meetings. It also contains the office where Vice Premier Kim Chaek died of a heart
attack in 1951.

American bombing raids targeted the site, inspiring one of
Kim Il Sung's more preposterous trumped-up charges. He
accused his own foreign minister, Pak Hon Yong, of coordi-
nating the bombings and sent him to the gallows.

108 • An Sang Taek Street

The regime has cultivated close ties with Koreans in Japan.
One of them, import-export trader An Sang Taek, built this
residential area in 1987. He was hailed for "services for the
prosperity and progress of the homeland."

Other "patriotic donations" from Koreans in Japan include
Pyongyang Gold Lane (a bowling alley) and Pyongyang Golf
Course. Like the housing on An Sang Taek Street, these luxury
recreation spots cater to the privileged classes, including Koreans from Japan who have resettled in the North.

Before World War II, a Chinese community inhabited this
neighborhood. In his memoirs, Kim Il Sung recalls visiting a
restaurant here as a boy and having to speak Chinese.

Chonsung Revolutionary Museum

■ **KOREANS FROM JAPAN**

In December 1959 the freighter *Mangyongbong-ho* set sail from Niigata, Japan. The stateless Koreans aboard it were finally heading home. Since World War II they had been stranded in Japan, victims of a diplomatic impasse between Japan and South Korea. Shrewdly, the North stepped in and offered to take in these Koreans. The passengers on this voyage of the *Mangyongbong-ho* were the first of 82,000 to repatriate to North Korea.

For the regime the repatriations were a windfall. The overseas Koreans brought with them much-needed technical skills. And by abandoning a capitalist country for a communist one, they handed the regime a propaganda coup.

The repatriates were richly rewarded, landing generous salaries, access to special shops, and the best housing. They were envied and resented by the local population – not least by those evicted to make way for the newcomers.

But many repatriates remained discontented. Even preferential treatment in North Korea could not match their former living standards. And most had come not out of communist convictions but to escape discrimination in Japan. To this day, the repatriates are closely monitored as political unreliables.

About 700,000 Koreans remain in Japan, one-third of whom side with the North. (These are organized into an association known as Chongryon.) Ironically, the capitalists among them help prop up the North's Stalinist economy. The regime extorts "patriotic donations" from entrepreneurs in return for decent treatment for their Korea-based relatives.

109 • Cemetery (Mount Chang)

While the Revolutionary Martyrs Cemetery grabs the spotlight, cemeteries for ordinary people remain in the shadows. U.S. intelligence reveals one sprawling burial ground on Mount Chang – the main public cemetery? – as well as several smaller ones dotting the city (see Pyongyang map, pages 94-95). Korean cemeteries are typically found on hillsides.

110 • Cemetery of Korean People's Army Heroes

Exact location unknown.

While the regime trumpets the body counts of its U.S. and South Korean foes, it has never released its own casualty figures from the Korean War. (Foreign estimates vary wildly, but the best guess is that 300,000 Northern soldiers died, compared to 225,000 South Koreans and 36,600 Americans.) Likewise, the regime avoids mentioning this and other Korean War cemeteries – perhaps because the long rows of gravestones belie the army's vaunted invincibility.

The remains of 14 servicemen here, brought home in 2002, bear witness to another conflict. They were killed while on a secret mission in Vietnam.

■ THE KPA IN VIETNAM

Pitting a communist North against a capitalist South, the Vietnam War inevitably drew comparisons to the earlier conflict in Korea. Indeed, both Koreas, locked in a standoff at home, reprised their conflict on Vietnam's battlefields. The South Korean army dispatched troops to assist the South Vietnamese. And several hundred North Korean MiG pilots served covertly in North Vietnam, intercepting U.S. fighter jets.

Kim Il Sung had been very public in offering troops to help the North Vietnamese. But the overture put Hanoi in an awkward spot, as it claimed to be fighting against foreign intervention. Thus, when North Vietnam accepted the pilots in 1966, both sides maintained the utmost secrecy. In 2001 North Korea finally acknowledged its intervention.

111 • Three-Revolution Exhibition

In former communist states, exhibition halls that once trumpeted the successes of socialism now host trade fairs. Not so North Korea's stalwart Three-Revolution Exhibition. Its pavilions display the country's achievements in heavy and light industry, technology, electronics, and agriculture.

The electronics pavilion highlights North Korea's "peaceful use of atomic energy" (no mention of its nuclear-weapons program). The agriculture pavilion displays farm equipment. (With rare self-deprecation, North Koreans recount the blundering birth of their tractor industry. In 1958 they copied a Soviet model, but at the test-drive it could only go backward.)

Three huge red granite flags commemorate the Three-Revolution Movement. In 1973 Kim Jong Il dispatched squads of Party activists across the country to further the ideological, technical and cultural "revolutions." When not providing technological assistance, the activists attacked practices deemed "un-Communist."

The Three-Revolution Exhibition opened in 1993, replacing an earlier exhibition on the same site.

112 • Changsan Revolutionary Site

The glorious accomplishments now credited to the young Kim Jong Il read like a recent exercise in creative writing. When Kim was chosen as leader-in-waiting, his official hagiographers had not yet fleshed out his resume. That would explain why, when this site opened in 1977, the regime ended up rhapsodizing over trifling deeds. At Changsan Kim merely took part in mass labor campaigns alongside other students. He planted trees in 1957 and took part in road construction work in 1961.

113 • Reformatory (Chunghung-dong)

This reformatory and two others in the Pyongyang area house juvenile delinquents detained for petty theft or vandalism. Such offenses are committed not only by the lower class but also by bored rich kids. Hooliganism is one of the country's few ac-

Changsan Revolutionary Site

knowledged social problems; it is also one of the few known expressions of dissent.

114 • Foreign Languages Publishing House

Since 1949 this publishing house has churned out state propaganda for export. Through such publications, Kim Il Sung waged his bid for leadership of the Third World.

A handful of foreign copy editors form part of Pyongyang's tiny expat community. In 1967 a Venezuelan editor, Ali Lameda, told his boss the propaganda was too far-fetched for foreign audiences. For his skepticism, Lameda was accused of being an imperialist spy. He was imprisoned for one year and kept under house arrest for another six.

115 • Victorious Fatherland Liberation War Museum

North Korea came out of the Korean War with a net loss of territory. So how can the regime call it the "Victorious Fatherland Liberation War"? The circle is squared as follows. At first, the North's war aim was to "liberate" the South, which it did (for a few months). But then came a UN counterattack, followed by a stalemate. The regime adopted a new war aim – preserving socialism in the North – and signed the armistice. Victory!

The same kind of spin-doctoring pervades this war museum. Exhibits accuse South Korea of launching the surprise attack on June 25, 1950, that triggered the war – yet the rest of the world knows that attack actually came from the North.

Rows of military hardware fill the museum. Proudly displayed are North Korean MiG fighter planes and the first tank to enter Seoul. U.S. planes and tanks, some badly damaged, sit in abject captivity.

The museum's huge cyclorama depicts the battle of Taejon. The North Koreans captured this strategic city on July 20, 1950, in what would be the Americans' greatest defeat of the war.

Opened near Haebang Hill in 1953, the museum moved to its present location in 1974.

■ AMERICAN ATROCITIES

The war museum's section on American atrocities conflates fact and fiction. It is true, as charged here, that the Americans waged war with little regard for civilians. Their indiscriminate bombings left the entire country in ruins.

Less convincing are accusations of germ warfare. U.S. planes, it's alleged, dropped insects carrying plague and cholera. Though jars full of insects are displayed as evidence, these charges are almost certainly fraudulent. The regime refused to allow the International Red Cross to investigate. Instead it presented sympathetic foreign scientists with prepackaged evidence, much of it suspect. For instance, though supposedly dropped from great heights, in sub-zero temperatures, the insects were found alive.

Finally, American soldiers are accused of massacring civilians – more than 35,000 in Sinchon County alone. Such charges are exaggerated, but some murders of civilians did occur. The available evidence suggests they were usually committed by South Korean, not American, troops. Nevertheless, the United States commanded all UN troops in Korea and was ultimately responsible for their conduct.

116 • Mokran House

Exact location unknown.
Mokran ("Magnolia") House boasts a massive hexagonal room where the Party's Central Committee holds receptions for foreign delegations. Among the dignitaries feted here was Russian president Vladimir Putin, who joined Kim Jong Il for a banquet in 1999. South Korean president Kim Dae Jung also gave a banquet here for Kim Jong Il.

117 • Korean Film Studio

Of the 30-odd feature films annually produced in North Korea, about two-thirds originate here. The Korean Film Studio

Victorious Fatherland Liberation War Museum

was founded in 1947. In 1949 it released the country's maiden film, *My Home Village*, a saga about the making of an anti-Japanese partisan. The studio's outdoor stage sets recreate locales as varied as a peasant's house, a landowner's mansion, and a street in old Seoul.

■ NORTH KOREAN CINEMA

The regime regards motion pictures as an "ideological weapon for class struggle" – a form not of entertainment but of indoctrination. Most feature films concern the anti-Japanese guerrilla war, the Korean War, or life under socialism. But whatever the setting, each film is laden with political sermonizing.

No known film has expressed even veiled criticism of the regime. Any shortcomings of socialism are shown to stem from overbearing low-level officials, who are then set straight by their Party superiors. In this way the regime distances itself from failed policies. For instance, *Guarantee* (1987) concerns a man maltreated by the authorities because he has family in South Korea.

An entire genre of "counter-intelligence films" glorifies the rule-by-terror of the secret police. Chillingly, these films urge viewers to "sharpen their revolutionary vigilance" – that is, to report on their fellow citizens. In 1957, amidst a Party purge, the first such film was released, with the ominous title *The Unfinished Battle*.

Kim Jong Il takes a special interest in film production and has written about its ideological uses. But Kim's cineaste pursuits had another, darker side. To improve the country's film industry, he allegedly masterminded the 1978 kidnapping of a South Korean movie star and her director husband. Choe Un Hui and Shin Sang Ok endured four years in prison before agreeing to make movies for the regime. The two escaped in 1986.

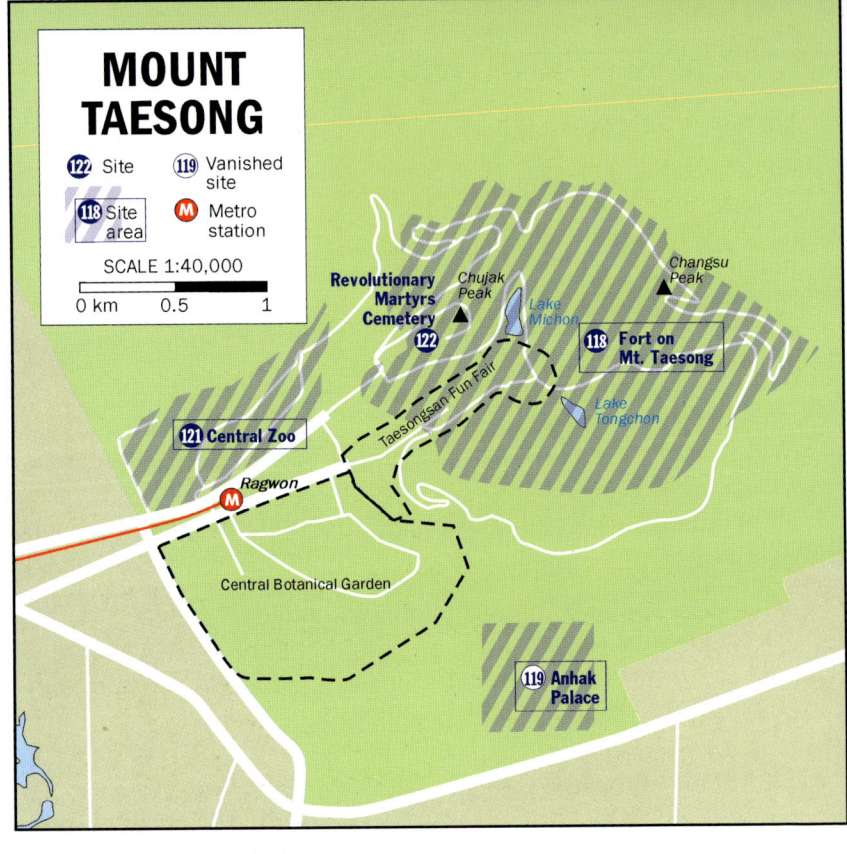

MOUNT TAESONG

122 Site **119** Vanished site

118 Site area **M** Metro station

SCALE 1:40,000

0 km   0.5   1

Revolutionary Martyrs Cemetery ▲

Chujak Peak

Lake Michon

Changsu Peak ▲

122

Taesongsan Fun Fair

118 **Fort on Mt. Taesong**

Lake Tongchon

121 **Central Zoo**

M *Ragwon*

Central Botanical Garden

119 **Anhak Palace**

Mount Taesong

A significant historic site, Mount Taesong is also a major recreational area for Pyongyangites.

118 • Fort on Mount Taesong

After being sacked in 246, the capital of Koguryo was relocated to Mount Taesong. In 427 this capital became permanent and was fortified with a 7-kilometer-long wall.

For centuries the site lay in ruins. Kim Il Sung accused the Japanese of damaging and looting the relics. But, as he admitted, the North Koreans also neglected the site, using ancient burial sites here as farms for livestock.

The main entrance to the fort – the impressive Nam (South) Gate – was rebuilt in 1978. The wooden original has been replaced by this concrete replica. Later renovations were financed by UNESCO, the UN cultural organization.

A "secret camp" used by Kim's guerrillas has allegedly been discovered on Mount Taesong, complete with the celebrated "slogan-bearing trees."

■ SLOGAN-BEARING TREES

One of the regime's more dubious claims is to have found trees carved with slogans by Kim Il Sung's guerrillas. At first, such discoveries were confined to the alleged guerrilla camp on remote Mount Paektu. Trees on Chong Hill, for instance, are said to have been carved in 1939 with slogans such as: "Korean youth, come out quickly and join actively in the anti-Japanese war!"

Then campaigns were held to discover more trees. Like splinters of the True Cross, thousands of these manufactured relics came out of the wood works. They were suddenly found on Mount Taesong and Mount Ryongak, places that were never known for guerrilla activity but were easily visited from Pyongyang. And the slogans were suspiciously prophetic, announcing that Kim would rule Korea and be succeeded by (the then-infant) Kim Jong Il!

Slogan-bearing trees are displayed both on-site and at the Korean Revolution Museum.

119 • Anhak Palace

Vanished site.
This 5th-century palace housed the royalty of the Koguryo

Dynasty. The complex consisted of more than 50 buildings, with government offices standing in front and the royal residences lying in the rear. Following the rules of geomancy, the buildings all faced south, and the main gate sat at the center of the south wall. The complex formed a perfect square, with walls that were each 622 meters long and stood up to 12 meters tall.

Kim Il Sung ordered the ruins excavated, a task that took more than a decade and required the eviction of local peasants. The hill, garden and pond on the grounds have been reconstructed. But foundations and roof tiles are all that remain of the vast palace itself. A model of it is displayed in the Korean Central History Museum.

120 • Kwangbop Temple

Exact location unknown.
This Buddhist temple dates back to 392, just after Buddhism was officially recognized in Korea. Destroyed by U.S. bombing in 1953, it lay in ruins for decades, not to be rebuilt until 1990. Though the regime has suppressed Buddhism, it has reconstructed a few ancient temples such as Kwangbop, acknowledging them as part of Korea's cultural heritage.

Foreign Buddhist tour groups are invariably brought to this

Nam Gate, Fort on Mount Taesong

temple. They are told that Kwangbop is a training center for Buddhist priests and monks. But some outsiders are skeptical. A South Korean source maintains the residents are actually state employees posing as monks. Whatever the truth, it's clear that the regime uses its Buddhists as a political tool to reach out to Koreans abroad.

121 • Central Zoo

Elephants are known for their longevity and thick skin. The pachyderms at this zoo demonstrated plenty of both: they survived a political attack by Kim Il Sung. Kim once objected that keeping elephants and other foreign creatures was typical of "capitalist" zoos. To bolster patriotism, he said, the Central Zoo should show animals native to Korea.

But when it opened in 1959, the zoo housed animals from the Soviet Union, China, Mongolia, and (in the elephants' case) Vietnam. And the imported beasts have remained. They have since been joined by rhinoceri from Zimbabwe, donated by Kim's ally Robert Mugabe.

After Kim's death, the dogs he kept at Kumsusan Assembly Hall were reportedly sent to the zoo. The fate of these privileged pooches, however, was nothing compared to that of the swans of Pyongyang's original zoo. They were cooked and eaten by hungry American soldiers during the Korean War.

122 • Revolutionary Martyrs Cemetery

Kim Il Sung's anti-Japanese guerrillas won acclaim as national heroes. Yet for many years their graves on Mount Taesong lay neglected. The usually infallible Kim publicly took the blame for this oversight. Soon after, in 1975, this cemetery was created. (In 1985 the cemetery expanded from about 60 graves to 110.)

The Revolutionary Martyrs Cemetery makes for an impressive tribute. Each revolutionary lies beneath a bronze bust and a plaque listing highlights of his or her career. A vast flag, carved in blood-red granite, serves as a backdrop. Piped-in funereal music adds gravitas.

Only Kim's closest comrades lie in this hallowed ground. Their graves are arranged in order of importance – not in the partisan struggle, that is, but in the political arena. With few exceptions, the most celebrated "martyrs," buried in the top row, did *not* die on the battlefield. They include Kim Il Sung's first wife, Kim Jong Suk; Vice-Premier Kim Chaek; and Armed Forces Minister O Jin U. All told, about one-third of those buried in the cemetery died after liberation.

Ironically, those guerrillas who gave their lives in battle have been relegated to less prominent graves in lower rows. Many fell in remote parts of Manchuria, and their bodies were never recovered – hence, their graves are empty. Moreover, some died without leaving behind so much as a photo of themselves. To fashion their busts, sculptors supposedly relied on Kim's descriptions of their faces.

■ THE ANTI-JAPANESE GUERRILLAS

Kim Il Sung's "Korean Revolutionary Army" commands an exalted place in the national pantheon. Kim called on the entire society to emulate the guerrillas, to learn from their militance and self-sacrifice. For instance, when faced with technical obstacles, high-rise architects read *Reminiscences of the Anti-Japanese Guerrillas* to boost their morale.

Glorifying the guerrillas proved politically shrewd. By crediting them, and not the Soviets, with liberating Korea, Kim could pursue a more independent foreign policy. And by describing them as the forebears of the army and Party, Kim settled domestic factional conflicts in his favor.

But the guerrillas' vaunted deeds do not stand up to scrutiny. They fought not from 1932 to 1945, as is alleged, but only from about 1936 to 1940. They were not an autonomous army but a wing of Chinese partisan forces. Most importantly, there is no evidence that they played any part in Korea's liberation.

Revolutionary Martyrs Cemetery

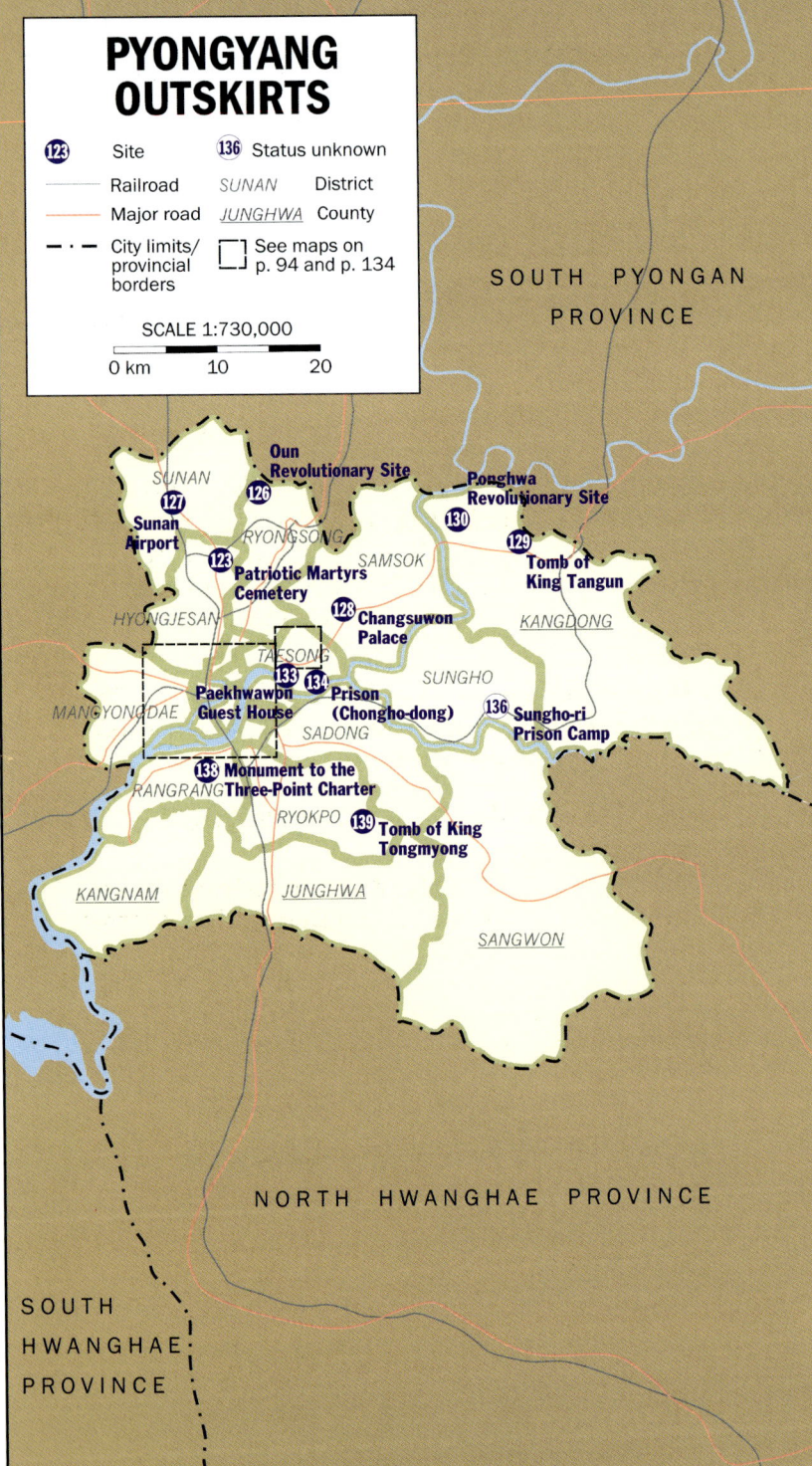

PYONGYANG OUTSKIRTS

123 Site
136 Status unknown
Railroad
Major road
City limits/provincial borders
SUNAN District
JUNGHWA County
See maps on p. 94 and p. 134

SCALE 1:730,000

0 km   10   20

SOUTH PYONGAN PROVINCE

SUNAN
127 Sunan Airport
126 Oun Revolutionary Site
RYONGSONG
130 Ponghwa Revolutionary Site
129 Tomb of King Tangun
123 Patriotic Martyrs Cemetery
SAMSOK
HYONGJESAN
128 Changsuwon Palace
KANGDONG
TAESONG
SUNGHO
133 134 Paekhwawon Guest House
Prison (Chongho-dong)
136 Sungho-ri Prison Camp
MANGYONGDAE
SADONG
138 Monument to the Three-Point Charter
RANGRANG
RYOKPO
139 Tomb of King Tongmyong
KANGNAM
JUNGHWA
SANGWON

NORTH HWANGHAE PROVINCE

SOUTH HWANGHAE PROVINCE

Pyongyang outskirts

123 • Patriotic Martyrs Cemetery

Laid to rest at Patriotic Martyrs Cemetery are almost 400 distinguished figures, including high officials, artists, and scientists. A South Korean source alleges that officials purged in the 1960s and 1970s are also buried here. (But why would they be buried with honors?)

Specific figures honored here include:

- Nationalist guerrilla **Yang Se Bong**, who was Kim Il Sung's commander in 1930.
- Secret agent **Kim Chol Ok**. During the Korean War, Kim was sent behind enemy lines to organize guerrilla units. His body was never recovered, and the grave is empty.
- **Choe Dok Sin**, a former South Korean foreign minister who, in 1986, executed a stunning about-face and moved to the North.

Unlike the exalted Revolutionary Martyrs Cemetery, this burial ground is rarely mentioned. It was completed in 1986. Kim Jong Il had portraits engraved on the headstones in 1998.

124 • Chinese People's Volunteers Martyrs Cemetery

Exact location unknown.
This cemetery in Hyongjesan District is the final resting place for 112 Chinese soldiers who fell in the Korean War. Another Chinese cemetery, in Hoechang County, east of Pyongyang, contains the grave of Mao Zedong's son Mao An Ying, killed in an American air raid. Chinese and North Korean officials lay wreaths at these graveyards each October 25 to commemorate China's entry into the Korean War.

125 • 125 Factory

Exact location unknown.
The output of 125 Factory has helped thrust North Korea onto the world's front pages. Defectors testifying before the U.S. Congress have identified this site in Hyongjesan District as a missile assembly plant. Nearby, in 1999, U.S. satellite photos recorded what appeared to be tests of the long-range Taepo-Dong 2 missile. Missile launch sites are allegedly maintained in Sangwon and Junghwa counties.

North Korea is a nightmare for nonproliferation efforts. The missiles it manufactures give it a means of delivery for the nuclear weapons it is developing. The danger is not confined to Northeast Asia: the regime is the world's largest exporter of ballistic missiles, supplying customers like Pakistan and Iran.

126 • Oun Revolutionary Site

In 1991 Kim Il Sung bestowed his position as supreme commander on his son Kim Jong Il. The hand-me-down uniform was no easy fit. Unlike most other males his age, the younger Kim had never served in the military. Nevertheless, the propaganda machine has labored overtime to tailor Kim Jong Il with the reputation of a warrior. The camp where Kim got six weeks of basic training in 1962 – his only brush with army life – has been turned into Oun Revolutionary Site.

127 • Sunan Airport

It was a minor military airstrip during the Korean War. But Sunan has since grown into Pyongyang's main airport. The airport still serves military functions: the Air Force Academy sits north of the terminal building, and the hills surrounding the airport bristle with clusters of anti-aircraft guns.

The suburb of Sunan was once known for its gold mines, and gold dredges are still visible in the area.

128 • Changsuwon Palace

In 1974 Kim Il Sung had this lavish villa built for Prince Norodom Sihanouk, the exiled leader of Cambodia. Topped with a Korean-style roof, the 40-room palace boasts high ceilings

어은혁명사적지

조선우표 DPR KOREA 1991 10전

Oun Revolutionary Site

Sunan Airport

dripping with chandeliers. At its heart is a vast ballroom where Sihanouk often entertained foreign diplomats. The interior was reportedly modeled on that of Kim's own residence (see "Kumsusan Memorial Palace," page 106).

The palace grounds include a private Buddhist temple and a gymnasium. It overlooks Changsuwon ("Lake of Longevity"), an artificial lake surrounded by wooded hills. It's not known whether Sihanouk uses the palace anymore.

■ PRINCE SIHANOUK

They were the odd couple of East Asian politics. Cambodia's Prince Sihanouk, a self-indulgent royal, and Kim Il Sung, a crusading communist, forged a friendship that defied all ideological explanation.

At times of upheaval in Cambodia, Sihanouk availed himself of Kim's hospitality. Ousted by the Khmer Rouge in 1975, the prince briefly sought refuge in North Korea. After Vietnam's 1979 invasion, Sihanouk fled his homeland again, shuttling between Beijing and Pyongyang. As Kim's guest he dabbled in movie production – all expenses paid by the state – before returning home for good in 1991.

The two leaders' close relationship puzzled observers. Sihanouk says he was moved by Kim's generosity. As for Kim, some believe he saw Sihanouk as a useful link to the non-communist world.

129 • Tomb of King Tangun

In 1993 the regime made a startling announcement. It claimed to have unearthed the skeletal remains of King Tangun, who

Tomb of King Tangun

was long considered a mythical figure. (Tradition holds that Tangun founded the Korean state in 2333 B.C.E. Then again, tradition also holds that his father descended from heaven and that his mother was a bear.)

The "discovery" was not as farfetched as it sounds. Some scholars abroad believe the Tangun myth may be loosely based on a real historical figure or figures. Furthermore, the site was identified as Tangun's tomb for centuries, although it was assumed to be merely a symbolic shrine.

Still, the claims gave skeptics plenty of ammunition. There was the suspiciously precise dating of the remains: 5011 years old, "plus or minus 267 years." Furthermore, the bronze artifacts unearthed could not predate the Bronze Age. (Thus one South Korean scholar speculates that the tomb is actually from the 6th or 7th century C.E.) The regime also accused the Japanese of writing Tangun out of the history books. But it is hard to see how falsehoods imposed during Japan's 35-year rule could have survived so long after liberation.

Was the discovery faked? Since Kim Il Sung ordered the excavation to prove Tangun's existence, the archaeologists may have had no choice but to find him. And after all, such a find provided vast political capital. By demonstrating that the Korean state originated in Pyongyang, the regime could claim legitimacy vis-a-vis South Korea. And by showing that the

Korean nation was older than the Japanese, the regime said the discovery bolstered Korea's "pride and honor." (Korean egos have long been bruised by assertions that the nation's culture was derived from Japan.)

Like the discovery itself, the renovation of Tangun's tomb sacrificed historical accuracy on the altar of national glory. Instead of refurbishing the original earthen tomb, the regime replaced it with a granite step-pyramid standing 22 meters tall. The new tomb on Mount Taebak was dedicated in 1994. Kim Il Sung was reviewing the blueprints for the tomb on the night he died.

130 • Ponghwa Revolutionary Site

The village of Ponghwa was home to Kim Il Sung's family in 1916-1917. Kim's father, Kim Hyong Jik, founded and taught at Myongsin School. A statue of the elder Kim was erected here, and in 1968 the place was designated a revolutionary site.

Kim Hyong Jik supposedly held secret meetings here with the Korean National Association, a pro-independence group. A small granite monument here, honoring Kim and other anti-Japanese figures, was allegedly erected in 1928. Could this monument be a fake? Scholars from abroad dismiss the notion that Kim played any meaningful role in the independence movement.

131 • Ponghwa Clinic

Exact location unknown.

Treatment at this clinic is available only to the Kim family and the highest officials. Patients receive high-standard medical care unavailable in the rest of the country. Ponghwa Clinic (also known as the "Government Hospital") opened in 1971. It is located in Ponghwa-ri, Kangdong County.

132 • Executive Apartments

Exact location unknown.

A declassified CIA report reveals the existence of the Executive Apartments. This closely guarded elite residential compound houses government ministers. It consists of four buildings, each two or three stories high, containing a total of 80 apartments. The Executive Apartments are located near Ponghwa Clinic.

133 • Paekhwawon Guest House for Foreign Dignitaries

This villa was a heartbreak hotel for several visiting statesmen. They came in the hope of influencing the regime but went home with empty promises.

- Former U.S. President **Jimmy Carter** came in 1994 to urge Kim Il Sung to freeze the country's nuclear program.
- In 2000, during the first inter-Korean summit, South Korean President **Kim Dae Jung** pressed Kim Jong Il here for North-South family reunions and economic cooperation.
- U.S. Secretary of State **Madeleine Albright** met Kim Jong Il here, appealing to him to abandon his ballistic missile program.

The name "Paekhwawon" means "one hundred flowers," referring to the blossoms on the grounds. The house, which overlooks the Taedong River, was built in 1983.

134 • Prison (Chongho-dong)

This unnamed prison, marked on a U.S. intelligence map, is one of Pyongyang's only known correctional facilities. The Ministry of Public Security asserts there are only three prisons in North Korea, holding no more than 1000 prisoners in all (see "Hyongsan Prison," below).

135 • Hyongsan Prison

Exact location unknown.
The regime has always been loath to discuss its political prisoners. Nevertheless, in 1995 it admitted to Amnesty International that it was holding 240 citizens for "anti-state activities," all at Hyongsan Prison. Given its name, perhaps this prison lies in Hyongsan-ri, 11 kilometers northwest of Taedong Bridge.

136 • Sungho-ri Prison Camp

Status unknown.
In 1994 South Korea said some of its citizens had been kidnapped by the regime and were being held in this camp. The charges were backed by Amnesty International. Former North Korean ministry officials also reportedly numbered among the camp's 600 prisoners. The regime denied having any such camp (some sources say it was relocated after its existence was revealed). Defectors say 100,000 to 200,000 political prisoners

are being held in camps across the country (see North Korea map, page 14).

137 • Cemetery of Soviet Servicemen

Exact location unknown.
In this burial ground rest the Soviets who helped free Korea from Japanese rule. North Korean and Russian dignitaries visit this cemetery in Sadong District each August 15, the anniversary of liberation. Neither this site, nor the Soviets' role in liberation, is publicized.

The Soviets took Pyongyang with little, if any, resistance: Combat in Korea was confined to the northeast. So how did these servicemen die? A foreigner who has seen the cemetery said many buried here actually worked as bureaucrats overseeing the Soviet occupation. Some succumbed to mosquito-borne encephalitis.

138 • Monument to the Three-Point Charter for National Reunification

This monument commemorates Kim Il Sung's proposal for reunifying Korea. Kim said that reunification should be achieved peacefully, without foreign involvement, and by transcending differences in ideology. He suggested a confederal state in which communism and capitalism would exist side by side.

1954
Laying wreaths at the Cemetery of Soviet Servicemen

**Monument to the Three-Point Charter
for National Reunification**

The three-point charter, announced in 1996, simply rehashes decades-old proposals. And for all its talk of peaceful coexistence, the North never stopped agitating for the overthrow of the South Korean government.

The monument was unveiled in 2001, at a "Grand Festival for National Reunification." Ironically, the event pushed the two Koreas even farther apart. South Koreans who attended the unveiling were accused by Seoul of politically aiding the North.

The 30-meter-tall monument straddles the southern approach to Tongil ("Reunification") Street. Two women in traditional dress, representing North and South, hold aloft the seal of the three-point charter. Bronze reliefs illustrate the three points and depict a joyous scene of reunification. Plaques of support are displayed from Koreans in the South and overseas. On a nearby stone slab appear Kim's instructions for reunification.

The monument was originally designed quite differently. It was to consist of a 55-meter-tall pillar, with three branches, representing Koreans in the North, South and overseas.

139 • Tomb of King Tongmyong

In the 5th century C.E., the Koguryo kingdom transferred its capital from what is now Jian, in China, to Pyongyang. The ancient state brought with it the remains of its founder,

Tongmyong. In his honor, a grave mound was built at this spot.

The tomb's interior suffered plundering during Japanese rule, leaving untouched only some frescoes and bronze rosettes. A further indignity was the 1993 renovation, which cluttered the site with faux ancient statues.

Surrounding the royal burial site are about 20 other tombs. Perhaps the most significant is Chinpa-ri Tomb No. 4. Covering its interior are paintings of animal-gods guarding the four directions of the compass (evincing Chinese influence).

140 • Cholbong-ri compound

Status unknown. Exact location unknown.
The regime's support for "worldwide revolution" goes beyond mere rhetoric, as was revealed in 1971. Mexican communists caught plotting a coup confessed to receiving guerrilla-warfare training in North Korea. Other insurgent groups from across the globe also acquired arms and training.

Foreign militants were housed (according to a South Korean source) at a compound in Cholbong-ri. Among them were the Japanese Red Army terrorists who hijacked a plane to Pyongyang in 1970. The regime gave them asylum, and despite Japanese pressure to extradite them, they remain in North Korea to this day.

Tomb of King Tongmyong

Note on sources

Recommended reading: Remarkably few Western-language sources exist on the city of Pyongyang. The article by geographers Alfred Schinz and Eckart Dege, "Pyongyang – Ancient and Modern – The Capital of North Korea" (*GeoJournal*, 22.1, 1990), is a useful exception to the rule. Additionally, Andrei Lankov gives a fascinating firsthand account of the city in the 1980s in "Pyongyang and Its People (Notes of a Soviet Student)," at www.fortunecity.com/meltingpot/champion/65/pyongyang_lankov.htm.

Even on North Korea as a whole, few works are reliable or informative. The definitive work on the political system is still the two-volume *Communism In Korea*, by Robert A. Scalapino and Chong-Sik Lee (Berkeley: University of California Press, 1972). A chapter on North Korea in *Korea's Place in the Sun*, by Bruce Cumings (New York: W.W. Norton & Company, 1997), also offers an intelligent, iconoclastic analysis of the roots of North Korea's political system. Helen-Louise Hunter has given North Korea watchers what they had long waited for: a reliable portrait of the country's society, in *Kim Il-Song's North Korea* (Westport, Connecticut: Praeger, 1999), adapted from a declassified CIA report. Another valuable account is *Human Rights in the Democratic People's Republic of Korea,* by Richard Kagan et. al (Washington, D.C., and Minneapolis: Asia Watch and Minnesota Lawyers International Human Rights Committee, 1988). Finally, in his biography *Kim Il Sung* (New York: Columbia University Press, 1988), Dae-Sook Suh assumes the daunting task of separating fact from fiction in the life story of the Great Leader.

North Korean sources: Despite their high ratio of propaganda to hard facts, North Korean sources on Pyongyang are among the most useful. Older sources tend to be more candid, for instance about Chinese and Soviet assistance.

The most informative English-language book about Pyongyang published in North Korea is *Pyongyang Review* (Pyongyang: Foreign Languages Publishing House, 1995). Valuable books about the country in English include *Do You Know about Korea?* (Pyongyang: Foreign Languages Publishing House, 1989) and Pang Hwan Ju and Hwang Pong Hyok's

Tourists Guide to Korea (Pyongyang: Foreign Languages Publishing House, 1994).

Useful periodicals include the monthly *Korea Today* and the pictorial *Democratic People's Republic of Korea.* The Korean Central News Agency, an official mouthpiece, publishes daily bulletins at www.kcna.co.jp.

South Korean sources: The Reunification Library, near the Kwanghwamun Post Office in Seoul, contains thousands of books on North Korea – mostly in Korean – but surprisingly little on Pyongyang itself.

Informative English-language sources from South Korea include *A Handbook on North Korea* (Seoul: Naewoe Press, 1998) and the periodical *Vantage Point* (Seoul: Naewoe Press). Tae Hung Ha's *A Trip through Historic Korea* (Seoul: Yonsei University Press, 1958) briefly describes pre-1945 Pyongyang. Also worth reading are the various publications of the Research Institute of National Unification, as well as the website of the National Intelligence Service, at www.nis.go.kr.

Other sources: This book relies in part on various North Korean, South Korean and American maps of Pyongyang. A Hungarian-language guidebook based on North Korean sources, Katalin T. Szentesi's *Koreai Népi Demokratikus Köztársaság* [*Democratic People's Republic of Korea*] (Budapest: Panoráma, 1987), proved informative. The German-language *Kleiner Reiseführer Nordkorea* [*A Small Guide to North Korea*] (Kiel, Verein zur Förderung regionalwissenschaftlicher Analysen, 1991), by Eckart Dege, supplements material from Schinz and Dege's *GeoJournal* article with coverage of specific sites in Pyongyang.

Aside from these published sources, valuable information came from former residents of Pyongyang, including Korean War refugees, foreign diplomats, and a defector.

Index of sites

Illustration credits

Front cover (both), 2-3, 5, 11, 12-13, 32-33, 38, 40, 42, 44, 47, 49, 50, 52, 53, 56, 57, 58, 60, 61, 62, 63, 65, 67, 68, 69, 71, 73, 74, 80, 81, 83, 84, 85, 86, 89, 93, 96, 98, 102, 103, 104, 106, 108, 111 (both), 112, 114, 115, 117, 125, 136, 139, 143, 144, 149, 150, 155, 156-157, back cover – taken by Eckart Dege between 1988 and 1996

16, 21, 23, 26, 28, 59, 78, 91, 147 – Hungarian National Museum

17, 18 – U.S. Department of Defense

22 – collection of Eckart Dege

25, 31, 79, 88, 105, 107, 113, 127, 129, 131, 142 – collection of Chris Springer

29 – collection of Gábor Osváth

39, 54, 55, 75, 76, 90, 100, 118, 120, 121, 148, 153 – taken by Chris Springer (39 and 100 taken 1995; all others taken 2002)

41 – Hungarian National Film Archives

Uncaptioned photos

Front cover: Children at Mansudae Grand Monument

Front cover inset: Guard at Revolutionary Martyrs Cemetery

2-3: View southwest from Tower of the Juche Idea

5: *Kayagum* players at Mangyongdae Students and Children's Palace

11: Cleaning Mansudae Grand Monument

12-13: View west from Tower of the Juche Idea

32-33: View northwest from Tower of the Juche Idea

150: Mother and daughter

153: Korean War veteran

155: Children on the march

156-157: Mural at Kaeson Revolutionary Site

Back cover: Ryugyong Hotel and Chollima Statue

The exhibition *Democratic People's Republic of Korea* features additional photos by Eckart Dege, plus images from 1950s North Korea. This exhibition was hosted by Galeria Centralis in Budapest in September-October 2002. An online version is slated to appear at www.osa.ceu.hu/galeria/catalog/2002/dprk/virtual/index.html.